The Spirit That Dreams

CONVERSATIONS WITH WOMEN ARTISTS OF COLOR

VOLUME ONE: IMAGE

JENÉ WATSON

INDIGO PEN

ISBN: 978-0-9977752-0-4

Library of Congress Cataloging-in-Publication Number: 2016948166

10 9 8 7 6 5 4 3 2 0 1 2 5 1 6

Printed in the United States of America

∞ This paper meets the requirements of ANSI/NISO Z39.48-1992 (Permanence of Paper)

Cover: Jenessa Sullivan, Trinidad and Tobago masquerade costume designer and fashion stylist. Photo used by permission.

For the old ones, the young ones, and all of us

Contents

Interviews are chronologically arranged

Memes

Acknowledgments

My mother, Janice, for my first hunt-and-peck typewriter as well as the computers on which much of this manuscript came together, for lending me her inner vision to help me see further, and for her unfaltering love. My aunts, Jo Ann and Barbara, for their prayers and encouragement so often sent through the mail. My brother, Wayne for his loyalty and humor that always reminds me of the richness of home. My brightly-shining son and little champ, Jared who has so many ways of showing his understanding of our other kinship—as makers, inquirers, and lovers of stories.

Mentor and friend, the stalwart artist Danny K. Russo, whose generosity and clarity of purpose continue to inspire. Friend and fellow librarian Dawn Wright Williams who is strong in her support of anyone and all things creative and Lylah Lockridge for casting her sharp eye over an early version of this text.

Family and friends whose major contributions during my crowd-funding campaign funded my stay at Vermont Studio Center, allowing me to make significant progress with this project: Mireille Agbossoumonde; H. Kofi Aifah; Wesley Bell; Jerrie Brooks; Garfield Bundy; James Esther, Jr.; Martha Ann Majors; Sharon Butler Martin; Katrina Perryman-Brown; L. J. Robinson, Jr. and Constance Whitehurst. Also, Georgia Lawyers for the Arts and attorney Heather McNay for legal advice.

The interviewees who, upon my reaching out via e-mail or approaching after a reading or screening, generously shared wisdom gained from their respective journeys. Jamil Bonnick and Lucious Smith for sticking with me as we hashed out layout and design and making this project look beautiful. Erica Hines Pereira, my always-cheerful Spanish language interpreter and translator. Illustrator Cannady Chapman, Yesha Darji, and artists who shared their work via Creative Commons. Readers for forgiving any errors that may have escaped my notice.

The Spirit That Dreams

Introduction

These women are vessels. And founts. They are a source. They preserve wisdom in the art of their lives, cultivating it in stories, in the way they move, in the paintings and pots they sculpt. They carry this knowledge in their bodies as they go about their tasks and the encounters of their days. And they pass it on.

~Rosemarie Freeney Harding, from Remnants: A Memoir of Spirit, Activism and Mothering

The Spirit That Dreams was many years in the making. I conducted most of these conversations while in my late twenties and early thirties to learn more about a small and random assortment of artists, some whose names will get many results if Googled or Bing-ed and others who are locally or regionally known. In some cases, I found out about the women's work by chance, while in others I deliberately sought it out.

The theme of this first of several short volumes is image. It focuses on artists who use painting, photography, and the moving image to tell their individual stories as well as our collective ones. You'll notice that the while the interviewees come from throughout the Afro-Atlantic world, the resources listed at the end of each volume of the collection are sometimes drawn from a wider range of cultures and continents. The same is true for the quotations and story interludes that form bridges between each of the interviews. With this extra reading and viewing material, I leaned toward straightforward portraits and (as often as possible) ones that allowed the artists to speak for themselves to give a more up-close and personal sense of their creative lives. For the benefit of those who are parents, teachers or otherwise connected to young people, I have included names of books for children—all of them biographical stories or fiction celebrating creativity in the lives of male and female protagonists.

For those wondering about the origin of the title: *The Spirit That Dreams* alludes to expressions of spirituality infused within the artists' work. Sometimes this is stated outright, and other times it's simply implied through the ways that the artists clear space in their works for reference to ancestors and tradition, personal healing, future survival, and community. I also sought to highlight the role that their sense of the sacred plays in helping them to achieve balance and fulfillment on a personal level.

"And what about the men?" my son asks as he chews his peanut butter and jelly sandwich and peers over my shoulder to read this text. It's true that this project would not have seen the light of day without the input of supportive men. Some of them invested financially. Others gave of their time and talent through contributing artwork or design skill. Some simply shared encouragement, conversation, and good vibes. Nevertheless, I wanted to document ways that women artists—the black and brown ones who are most often from working-class backgrounds—find the will and inspiration to get their work done alongside the hands-on job of taking care of children, other family and community. While there are some brother artists who share these concerns and responsibilities, more often such work falls squarely on women's shoulders, which makes the pattern by which we arrange our lives significantly different.

This dream that you hold in your hands has changed shape many times. It puts voices of women of color front and center and yet is an offering to all with the ears to listen and hearts to hear. It's a gift to the ones just setting out on their own creative journeys as well as those who want to head in new directions. As you read, I hope that common threads become visible to you and that they're useful in binding the stories told here to the ones that hold your own lives together. Please take your place among us and enjoy.

Little by little, the bird builds its nest.

-Haitian proverb

Eliciana Nascimento

Filmmaker

Independent filmmaker and media activist Eliciana Nascimento was born in Brazil's northeastern state of Bahia, a place recognized as the heart of Afro-Brazilian history and culture. Now a resident of California's Bay Area, Eliciana founded Candace Cine Video through which she creates films that center on memory and identity. Her earliest film credits are as co-producer of the documentary *Rhythmic Uprising* which depicts the methods that Afro-Brazilian cultural leaders use to uplift their communities and director of *Hip Hop in Seven Lives* which shows the positive impact that hip hop is having on the lives of urban youth in Brazil.

Supporters saw such promise in Eliciana's cinematic vision that they contributed to a crowdfunding campaign to help bring her most recent work *The Summer of Gods*, from concept to completion. Set in a pristine coastal village in her home state, this twenty-minute short film pays homage to Eliciana's maternal line including her great-grandmother who was a healer in the Yoruba tradition as well as to her mother whom Eliciana remembers as having extraordinary storytelling gifts. Since its release in DVD and digital download, many grassroots and global venues have screened *The Summer of Gods*, including the 2014 Cannes Film Festival Short Film Corner, the 2014 Bioneers Conference, the New York African Film

Festival 2015, Chicago's 2015 African Diaspora International Film Festival and the Encontro de Cinema Negro Zózimo Bulbul, the largest black film festival in Brazil.

The following interview was conducted by telephone on Sunday, June 7, 2015.

JW: Can you tell me when you were born and what you dreamed of being when you grew up? Did you always have it in mind to become a storyteller, a filmmaker?

EN: I was born in 1984, and I wanted to be two things. I wanted to be a teacher. I didn't know what I was going to teach, but I always like the idea of being in front of people and being able to teach something. And I also wanted to be an artist. I was involved in a theater group for most of my adolescent life and adulthood. I didn't dream about being a famous actress, but I wanted to be able to be involved in performing arts in some way. Eventually, I discovered cinema, and filmmaking became my main dream.

JW: Were you involved with the theater group that Abdias do Nascimento started or a different one? Please tell me about it.

EN: I wasn't involved with that one. I think that his group was popular from the 1940s into the 1960s. I know that [he was the inspiration for] the theater groups that a lot of us in the Black Movement started.[1]

My theater group was called Bem Me Quer. In Portuguese, it's the nickname for a type of wildflower. In Brazil, education is lacking. People living in poor communities

---

[1] For more on the relationship between civil rights and theater in Brazil and the US, see the Black Women of Brazil blog post "The Solano Trindade Popular Theater Celebrates 40 years" and Woodie King, Jr.'s documentary Black Theater: The Making of a Movement.

don't have access to a lot of things. So, community organizers just create organizations to be able to teach others to think about themselves in a better way and to try to find a better path in life, to have some kind of aspiration. It's usually a nonprofit or connected to some social movement. You know, a group of artists who get together and create something.

And that's what happened to me. I was just involved in a lot of social movements and nonprofits. I was doing theater and participating in performing arts as a way to find inspiration and find my way to knowledge, because I didn't have that at home.

JW: Did you stay with Bem Me Quer for a long time, or did you get involved with different theater organizations?

EN: I started with that group through my public school when I was twelve. Eventually, I became an arts educator with that group when I went to college. So, I went through three phases with them. One as someone who

needed help from the organization, then as an assistant to the professor and later when they hired me as an educator for the new group of adolescents that were part of the program.

JW: That's awesome. And it feeds right into my next question, which is about college. You were in college in the early 2000s. By that time, hadn't the number of blacks in Brazilian colleges increased a lot over the previous ten or fifteen years? Still, from what I understand, it's still hard for black people to access a university education and in turn a wide range of careers. Can you talk to me about your path from elementary school through high school and then on to college? What pushed you toward your dream?

EN: I think I was just a weird kid (chuckles). I always liked to read. I read a lot from the time I was little. My mom worked for a woman who became my godmother. She used to go to my godmother's house to clean because that was my mom's job. And I would go into their library and read all the books

Eliciana Nascimento

that I could. Also, I watched my godmother's kids who were all going to good schools. One became an engineer. The other became a doctor. And I wanted to be like those people. I made a comparison between what I saw at home, what I saw on TV and what I saw at [my godmother's] house. I noticed that the successful people read and studied. So, when I was little I said to myself that I needed to study and try to do my best. I didn't have a model or anyone who could guide me and take me by the arm and say, "This is the time to apply for this scholarship" or "This is what you need to do." I kind of just went with the flow and used the social movement projects and lessons that I got from those educators and people who were already in college. I started building my life through that.

And I agree that the number of black Brazilians going to college is increasing now, but education in Brazil is…You know that there is the slogan that Brazil is a racial paradise, that we don't have racism. But it's a lie, because education is one of the ways that racism is made stronger. We have the public school system which is really bad. Really bad. And basically, we don't learn much because the teachers are not taught to really give time to us or believe in us. So, the public school system is basically for poor people and black people, whereas the white community can afford to go to private schools, and they learn everything that they need to learn.

For the college level, it's a different system. The public universities—which are free—are the best ones. They are better than the private universities because the private universities are a way for [the people who run them] to make money. They're not as sophisticated. The public universities are

---

¹ *The vestibular is a rigorous and competitive test that covers math, science, history, literature, and foreign language and is taken over many days. Results are a major part of what determines admittance to a college or university.*

My mom would often dream that she would win the lottery and buy a house for us. That was her biggest dream. Anything else seemed out of our reach.

accredited, and everyone wants to go to them. But then, we have the vestibular that you need to pass[2]. If you went to a public school for your whole life, everyone knows that you won't have enough knowledge to be able to do well on the test. So, usually only wealthy whites can get into the public universities.

But then, the Black Movement is strong. Over the years, it's been able to achieve so much. We now have a system of quotas. [Brazilian] laws have changed so that now we have affirmative action similar to what you guys have here in the United States.

And because of affirmative action, more people of color have been able to attend public universities. This wasn't the case at the time that I attended college, but I do see a difference. Also, people are just becoming more aware that they need higher education, and they're enrolling in private universities getting themselves in debt to go to college.

JW: Can we go back a little? How old were you when you started helping your mom do domestic work? Did you help out until you graduated high school?

EN: We helped our mom with her jobs from the time we were little, from the time I was probably about ten or twelve. The owner of that company had a huge, fancy house. And he was always throwing parties. My mom would take us to those parties, and I would go there and help her to serve the guests. So, I was often in wealthy environments around people who had education and money. I was there working for them and observing and thinking, "Why can't we be like these people?" And that added to my will to do something different with my life.

JW: We've talked a lot about you being one of the first in your family to pursue extensive formal education. Many artists of color for whom this is true say that their parents expect them to use their education to help them get ahead financially by becoming doctors, lawyers, business people or to work in some other career of prestige. You decided to make films. Does your family think you're crazy?

(Laughter from both)

EN: I think my family always thought I was crazy, that I'm the "different" one. I think [I was spared the pressure because of] the fact that they didn't have much formal education or ambition and didn't know what we could be. Nobody else in the family really went to college, so no they didn't insist that I become a doctor, lawyer, or business person. My mom would often dream that she would win the lottery and buy a house for us. That was her biggest dream. Anything else seemed out of our reach.

I actually received the opposite message from my father. When I got accepted to college in Brazil, I was fortunate to get accepted to both a public university and private one. I got a scholarship to attend the private university. And because I'd fallen in love with theater, I wanted to study it in a public university and communication in the private one. Pursuing these two majors was what I wanted to make me happy with my life. At the time, my father had moved away to São Paulo to find work. A lot of people in Bahia go to São Paulo, the big city, with the hope of finding a better job and making more money. So, my dad had moved there, and we called him to see if he could send me money to help. He told me—and I don't even know how to exactly translate what he said into English. What he said was something like, "Only people who can afford to should go to college. If you can't afford it, just don't go." It was so obvious to him, and he wondered why I was trying to do something that was apparently not meant for me. Some people are not even fortunate enough to be able to enroll in *one* college, and I was trying to enroll in *two*!

My mom gave me a lot of incentive and she had a lot of hope for me, but there wasn't much else that she could do. I actually kind of motivated her to go back to high school after she was way older—somewhere in her forties—so that she could have something that she achieved in life. She'd said to me that she didn't want to die cleaning people's houses,

and I said, "Let's do something to change that." And I helped her to get her diploma.

JW: So, how many were in your family?

EN: My mother, my father, my sister, and my brother. I'm the youngest. Later, my father had a daughter from another relationship. So, I also have one half-sister.

JW: To my knowledge, you're the only Afro-Brazilian filmmaker—woman or man— who has translated some of the everyday life stories of Brazil and made them available to English-speaking viewers here in the States. Getting the Afro-Brazilian experience translated into English is rare. Did you set out to do this and how do you feel about it?

EN: Wow. I love that I'm a pioneer in something (laughter)! I think it happened because doing my MFA in Cinema here, I was always inclined to tell the story of my people. I didn't want to come to the US and just try to become Afro-American. I mean, I *am* an American. Not North American, but Brazilian. And I just thought it would be nice to tell the story of my people because Americans here—many of them—are so isolated. Since English is a language that is spoken in so many countries, they think they don't need to know much about other people. A lot of people think that the US is the center of the world. I felt that I needed to bring my culture and my story to create a consciousness and conversation about what's happening. It's not that what's happening here in the States is not important. But I think it's important for people here to learn about other places, other cultures so that then they'll be able to make a comparison between our experiences. That was my intention.

So, in my program we had to make two films, and in my first one I went to Brazil to shoot it. [*On the Day Matthew Was Born*] is about police brutality, because when I came from Brazil to the US I had been participating in movements to speak up about police brutality. We had so many friends who were not even criminals yet who had been shot by the police. They were just normal people. I wanted to share that issue that is a problem in Brazil that's also happening here. I think it's important to have this sense of community, how black people in different countries experience similar situations. And *The Summer of Gods* was about the *orixá*[3] experience that I wanted to be able to share. I don't know if I answered your question.

JW: You did. Absolutely. I do want to go back to something that you said just now. I've heard so many people from many points in the diaspora express this idea of Americans believing that they're the center of the world. Yet, what the rest of the world may see as a general American attitude is not necessarily one shared by all of those born in the US

---

[3] *Orixá (Brazil), orisha (Spanish speaking Latin America), and orisa (Nigeria) are alternate spellings for the Yoruba pantheon of natural energies or spirits.*

After my mom passed, I became more interested in the religion because I knew that that was a point of connection with her, where our souls met.

Certainly, over the years you have some blacks here who've developed arrogance or acceptance of certain behaviors. But historically, most of us saw world affairs in a way different from the dominant view. There are so many Americas, so many parts to the American experience even right here within these borders. Do you feel more a sense of kinship or more of a sense of separateness from the communities of color that you've come in contact with here, and when you screen your films what's been the reaction of the different people who get to see your work?

EN: I've actually been experiencing a lot of the African American community here, and I'm amazed. I think there is a kinship and a lot of people have so much interest and knowledge of other countries and what's going on outside of the US What I had in mind earlier was my university and how the views were often so limited to the US [Our curriculum focused] on film that was made here, and I wanted to bring something different for people to be able to see and experience. When I was fundraising for *The Summer of Gods* I got so much support. This film is a true, true expression of love within the community because I didn't have money to make the film, so I created a Kickstarter crowdfunding campaign. I had so many people from throughout the world to make contributions. A lot of people wrote to me saying, "This film needs to be made. We don't have films about *orixás* and we don't have films showing kids how they need to believe in our traditions." I felt embraced in the US and so many other countries. People wrote to me and are continuing to write to say that they see themselves or their daughters in the film.

JW: Can we talk about your mother a little more? She was part of Candomblé or Umbanda, and you weren't involved early on. But after she passed away, you decided to be initiated, though not in Brazil. You instead selected another point in the Diaspora—Cuba—as the place to receive your rites. Why Cuba instead of Brazil and what some of the differences and similarities were between the spiritual expressions you grew up with at

home and what you connected with in Cuba?

EN: That's a long and interesting story. When I was growing up, my mother would often take us to her hometown, in a rural area of Bahia to a little town named Ituberá. Her grandmother, my great-grandmother, lived there and used to tell us stories about her parents being slaves. She's over a hundred years old and still alive today. She lived on a small island that we could only access by boat. So, the story of Lili, the main character of *The Summer of Gods*, is very close to the experience I had during my childhood. When we were on vacation at my great-grandmother's house, I would listen to her stories and see her doing ceremonies to the spirits. I was very little and not very aware of what was going on when I was seeing these things. My mother also used to do things like the *mesa branca* where a group sits around a circular table covered in white cloth and talks to the spirits.

Eventually, I saw my mother participate in a pre-initiation ceremony for Candomblé.

If for some reason a person was not ready to fully commit, they did this kind of ceremony. One day when I was around seven or eight years old, I went with my mother and my sister to a ceremony where we stayed the whole night. The [pre-initiates] did all that they needed to do. The [elders] did a [spiritual] cleaning of my mother. And then the next day, all I remember is that I went back to my great-grandmother's house dressed all in white. I went there dressed in normal clothes, and came back in white clothes that didn't belong to me. They had to change my clothes to participate in the ceremony. And that's part of my film. The white clothing belongs to the magical world that the spirits guide Lili to.

I was never invited to be initiated until after my mother passed. My mother had a role. She was supposed to be a priestess, take care of other people and do the work, but she didn't get fully initiated. Because of the racism and all the discrimination against our religion in Brazil, a lot of people are very afraid of doing what they need to do.

JW: Still? It seems that the tradition is now kind of fashionable. Many people flaunt the white dresses and the *elekes* and head wraps. I didn't know that there was still as much stigma as there once was.

EN: A lot of people are now embracing the traditions, talking about them and showing value for what we have. But some are afraid. A lot of people lie about their religion because they are afraid of the discrimination they're going to suffer or that people are not going to see them the same way. So, my mother didn't become the priestess she was supposed to be. Before I came to the US, there was a priest who used to take care of me and my mother, but then he moved away. So, we never got to be part of what they call in Brazil an *ilé*, an ancestral house where you go to be initiated and where you participate in a community. I was always interested in learning more, getting the readings, and doing the cleansings. I wanted to know more, especially because I was involved with the Black Movement, and they valued the religion. I felt the call, but no one was taking me.

A year after I moved to California, my mother passed away. She was about forty-eight. When she passed, I went back to Brazil and wasn't sure about what I was going to do, if I was going to stay there or go back to the US I got accepted to an MFA program in San Francisco, so I decided to return to California for my studies. It was during this time that I found the House of Orishas, and it surprised me. I always thought that the *orixás* were only worshipped in Africa and Brazil. I didn't know much about the diaspora, didn't know much about Cuba or Haiti. But I started learning more and saw a lot of similarities between our traditions in Brazil and other places.

After my mom passed, I became more interested in the religion because I knew that that was a point of connection with her, where our souls met. I kept doing the steps that I needed to do until I had the opportunity to be initiated. And the family that I became connected to here in the US was [part of a spiritual family from] Cuba, and they took me there. When I got to Cuba, I went to a small town called Matanzas that looks just like Ituberá. Just like my mother's hometown. I was like, "Oh my gosh! This is home!" And the people were so humble and so simple. And my godfather in Cuba looked just like my grandfather, my mother's father. It was like I had a version of my family in Cuba.

Before I went to Cuba, one of the spiritual people who was taking care of me and my mother in Brazil, she passed away as well. This was one year after my mother died. So, basically, I'd lost my spiritual connection in Brazil. I couldn't just go back to Brazil and easily [receive my rites]. It's not done like that. It's like getting married. You have to build a family relationship. It's like falling in love and building a relationship. So, that's what happened. I found people that I felt safe with, who I thought I would work with. I trusted them. And I did the ceremony. Before they do the actual receiving of the *orixas*, they have a spiritual mass for your ancestors who must give you permission to go further. The leaders of the ceremony—who didn't know me—told me, "You come from very far away. You come from two different lands." Of course, that was Brazil and the US they said, "Your mother was supposed to be a priestess and she passed away when she was still young. Now, you're here to accomplish something that she couldn't." So I said, "Okay, I'm doing the right thing."

The lesson for me was that our ancestors walk with us. We were taken from Africa across the Atlantic, but we're still the same people, the same community. It doesn't matter if some are called African American, some are called Cubans or other people are called Brazilians. There is a connection, and I saw it when I went to Cuba. It was home.

JW: Is your great-grandmother still lucid? Since she's over one hundred years old, does she still know who you are and how does she feel about you now being part of this spiritual lineage?

EN: She's lucid, but she hears very little and sees very little. So, it's very hard to communicate with her. Before, she used to tell us stories. She knows that I'm my mother's daughter. When I go home, she pats my hand and knows my name. She is lucid. She tells me her dreams and that I need to do a mass for my mother. It's just hard to get into a deeper conversation with her because she can't hear much. So, it's really hard to talk now.

JW: We've talked a lot about *The Summer of Gods* and it being your way of paying respect to Bahia, nature and people like your mom and great-grandmother who keep the traditions alive. It really is a beautiful short film. Documenting these beliefs, honoring them and shining positive light on them is so important because it can help to teach those who may have misconceptions. At the same time that exposure can preserve, it can make

> *Cinema is a tool that I use to call for justice or just to share beauty. If it weren't through cinema, I'd probably do it through music if I could sing or art if I could paint. That's what I am.*

these traditions very vulnerable. What do you think about this? Do you ever feel a conflict between sheltering and exposing ancestral spiritual lessons and practices?

EN: No, I never feel a conflict. It's already vulnerable, because I know that some people don't know about our tradition. Or people who [think they do] know the wrong thing, and it's because other people have been speaking about what we do and have been doing so in the wrong way. If you see films that Hollywood has made popular about [this path], it's just not the right message. Just look at what people still think about voodoo. To them, it basically means witchcraft and negativity. People think of needles and voodoo dolls reducing our whole tradition to an artifact that you can get to do bad things to someone. We can't be silent about what we do and allow other people to talk about it in the wrong way.

JW: Beautiful. I'd like to talk for a minute

about cross-cultural film inspirations and influences. Like many people in the African Diaspora, I've loved Brazil for years. Carlos Diegues helped make Brazil real to me. His films threw me heart and head into the music, history, and spirituality of Brazil. Visually, your film *The Summer of Gods* reminds me of *Beasts of the Southern Wild*. In terms of message, it puts me in the mood of Julie Dash's *Daughters of the Dust*. Were these inspirations at all? Who are some of the other filmmakers or other storytellers who've captured your attention?

EN: It's nice that you mentioned Diegues. I really love his work. He's the first filmmaker who, you know, captured the Afro-Brazilian experience. I did research on blacks in Brazilian films and watched a lot of his films and love them. Diegues is one my inspirations, but I didn't think about him or any of his specific films when I did *The Summer of Gods*. And it's funny that you mention *Daughters of the Dust*, because someone recently wrote

an article with a title that was something like "Eliciana and the Orisha Cinema." The writer was saying that I'm someone who is helping to create a category, a new genre. It mentioned Diegues. And they kind of made a connection between *Daughters of the Dust* and *The Summer of Gods*. I did watch *Daughters of the Dust* a while ago, back when my English was really bad. I need to watch it again now that I understand a little more. I see connections between *The Summer of Gods*, *Daughters of the Dust*, and *Beasts of the Southern Wild*, but when I wrote the film, I didn't have any of those films in mind. It was basically my pure experience of going to my great-grandmother's house and experiencing her stories and the spirits and my later initiation into the tradition.

Before I wrote the script, I wrote my personal story and read it in class. My classmates said that I should really make it into a film because it's really touching and magical. Even though I didn't have Julie

Lili and Elegguá, *The Summer of Gods* (2014)

Dash's work in mind, since I was in academia I had to look for [previous films made by others] to support my project. *Daughters of the Dust* was one of the films that I used as a reference, especially the parts where it talks about the Unborn Child, which is a spirit. I mirrored that character with Elegguá as well as with my character Lili. Initially, I wasn't trying to create a connection, but I'm happy that there is one!

And with *Beasts of the Southern Wild*, it's really weird because I found out about that film only after my script had been approved and I'd already a whole semester of going through workshops and getting my script done. I was telling a friend about *The Summer of Gods* and she was like, "That sounds so much like *Beasts of the Southern Wild*." I said, "What is that?" and she told me. It was still playing in theaters, so I was able to see it here in San Francisco.

JW: Your short film *On the Day Matthew Was Born* is filmed in a favela and opens with a dedication to victims of police brutality. Do you set out to make "socially responsible cinema"? And is your Brazilian audience upset that you're exposing shameful topics to a foreign audience or are most of them happy that you're using your platform to tell important stories like this?

EN: For me, cinema is a tool that I use to call for justice or just to share beauty. If it weren't through cinema, I'd probably do it through music if I could sing or art if I could paint. That's what I am. I grew up participating in social movements and black movements. I see the problems of Brazil and also the problems of black people in Brazil. And not only Brazil but other countries, and it's such a problem that innocent people are killed just because they're black. The racism is still there. I just have to talk about it. So, yes, it's my intention to make political films or films that talk about topics not well-covered in the media like our traditions and spirituality.

As far as [audience response], I think we're talking about two different types of Brazilians. There are the ones who are with me and believe that we need justice and that we need to educate the public. And there are the elites who pretend that everything is fine, that Brazil is happy and the land of *carnaval*. They were raised with access to all of the opportunities that they needed. I don't think that they would even go to theaters to see my films because they don't care. And that's okay. I'm making films to talk about the issues that I need to talk about, and I am discovering my audience as I progress in my career. I'm finding people not just in Brazil or the US but all over the world. I have people writing to me from the Netherlands, Greece—places that I didn't even know that people knew about *orixás*—and wanting to do screenings. I'm like, "Wait a minute—*orixás* in Greece? Seriously? I didn't know!" I'm happy to find these people and that they're able to find my work and that it's speaking to them, you know? I want to keep working and making films that are impactful to our communities in some way.

JW: Tell me about your creative process. About how long, in general, does it take you to take a vision from a seed of an idea to a fully developed one? And time wise, how do you balance your personal projects, these creative stories that you want to tell with the ones that you tell for your commercial clients? Are you able to earn your living from your creative projects alone?

EN: Good question. It's really hard (laughs). I say that I have three lives. One is the life of a normal human being who has to work, and pay the bills. That means

going to work and earning the money to pay my student loans, pay my rent and survive. I have the life of being a filmmaker and participating in screenings when I can, editing the films, building my website, answering people's e-mails, participating in interviews like the one I'm having with you now. And then there's my spiritual life. I'm a *santera*, and this is something that I have to keep working at. I need to keep studying, taking care of my spiritual self and helping people when they come to me. I have to keep a balance between everything.

The time that it takes me to complete a project all depends. *On the Day Matthew Was Born* and *The Summer of Gods* were projects for school, so I had a timeline. The first one took one year from writing the idea to completing the film. The second one took me a year and a half from the time I came up with the idea to making it available on DVD. For that one, I had to raise money. It was a bigger film, a bigger project. Now, I have three projects in mind. With one, I have the first draft fully written. The other one is a small idea, and the other is a big idea. And I'm trying to decide which one I should work with first. And I'm still distributing *The Summer of Gods*. So, I don't know how long it's going to take me to work on my next project. It's all going to depend on having the funds ready. I'm still trying to create that balance.

I try to manage my day by waking up very early. I'm a meditator, so I get up at about 5:30 in the morning. I do my spiritual reading and study. Then I go to work, come back home and I try to work on my films. You know, I answer e-mails and sell my films and do what I have to do. Now, I have to find a place in my life to work on the next project—which is writing the script, looking for funds and all that kind of stuff. I'll probably do it on weekends when I should be having fun (laughs).

JW: Final question—When the time comes and you're standing in the same position as your great-grandmother looking over your life, what do you want to see? What's your grand vision for your life, the legacy you want to leave as a woman and creative person?

EN: Wow. That's an awesome question. I've always believed that everything has a reason, and this must be why I said to myself that I should do this interview today. I think I still need to do more work in Brazil, especially with young women. There is a big problem there with early pregnancy. A lot of girls are getting pregnant at thirteen or fourteen. This is on the social level. I want to go back to Brazil at some point and help guide these girls towards a better life.

On the spiritual level, I know that I have to take care of a lot of people and that I'm going to be responsible for initiating people in the traditions. So, another one of my main roles is going to be to become a mama, a spiritual guide, and to learn more about the religion and traditions of our ancestors, help keep them alive.

Lili and her grandmother, *The Summer of Gods* (2014)

I can look back on my work and be inspired by France, Haiti, Africa, the Black experience, and Martha's Vineyard... and admit: there is no end to creative expression.

- Loïs Mailou Jones

Photo Credit: Janis Wilkins

Laura James
Painter

Laura James is a self-taught painter whose work is largely based on depictions of religious icons and dramatic scenes from the Bible. This creative path emerged after the Brooklyn-born artist chanced upon a book titled *Ethiopian Magic Scrolls* displayed in the window of one of her neighborhood's *botanicas*. The Tawahedo (Ethiopian Orthodox) tradition detailed in the books' pages is one of the oldest Christian lineages in the world.

Ironically, though women are forbidden from physically entering some of the most ancient and sacred of Ethiopia's churches, Laura's indirect study of their mysteries has allowed her to convey her subjects in a potent style that is nearly indistinguishable from the best of the orthodox tradition. In recognition of her mastery of this form, the Catholic Church commissioned Laura to illustrate a *Book of Gospels.* Since its release by Liturgy Training Publications in 2000, this lectionary has been used by an array of Christian congregations hungry for more culturally-inclusive religious imagery.

A New Yorker of Caribbean descent, Laura warmly embraces cultural fusion and includes sacred figures Buddhist, Hindu, and Yoruba traditions in her body of work. In 2016, she began working on illustrations for the Tradewinds Publications children's book *Boonoonoonous Hair* with noted Jamaican author, Olive Senior. It is the second picture book collaboration between the two, the first being *Anna Carries Water*. In 2014, she co-founded The Bronx 200, a directory of artists from a wide array of ethnicities and working in diverse media, its aim being to "create a new platform for visibility and community building in the Bronx and beyond." In Fall 2016, Hachette Book Group will release her adult coloring book illustrating the 46 parables of Jesus.

Laura and I began the following exchange via e-mail in the summer of 2013 and concluded it in winter 2013.

JW: What were you like when you were younger? Did you dream of pursing art as a career?

LJ: I didn't talk much. I read a lot, and the Brooklyn Public Library was one of the few places my parents would let my sister and me go alone. So we went there a lot! I love to read. I've learned so much from books. They are really my teachers. I liked to read books by black authors. I remember reading Toni Morrison's *The Bluest Eye*, *Plum Bun* by Jessie Redmon Fauset, and Ann Petry's *The Street*. I borrowed books like Baldwin's *Giovanni's Room* and *If Beale Street Could Talk* as well as Mary Helen Washington's

Black Eyed Susans [and Midnight Birds]. I also remember reading Adrienne Rich and Gabriel Garcia Marquez. My mother taught me to sew and crochet, so I liked to do that. I also taught myself to play the piano, and I liked to sing.

My first idea of what I would do as a job was working with computers. This was probably around the seventh grade. At this time, computer science was suddenly "a thing," and I was really interested in them because they were so new and a lot of people didn't know how to use them. We used them in school, and my cousin was sort of a computer nerd and had one at home. When

"Self Portrait as Frida Kahlo," Laura James

the time came, I applied to a lot of different high schools, including one named Murray Bertram, which was supposed to have a good computer program at the time. But I also applied to La Guardia, the school from the movie *Fame*, and was accepted for a few of the programs. After that, I basically gave up on computers!

In high school, I started a magazine with a group of friends called *The Black House* where we focused on poetry and social issues as well as art and photography. Through the years, I was also occasionally involved with different groups of artists to organize exhibits.

JW: I came across your work by chance on the internet when doing a Google image search for Ethiopian sacred art. Even though your work is beautifully bound to that tradition, it also seems to pay tribute to the visual traditions of Haiti. For you, was this a subconscious or intentional fusion? When you were teaching yourself technique, did you study the self-taught artists of Haiti, too?

LJ: I've always liked looking at a lot of different kinds of art. For visual art, my first loves were Leonor Fini, Natalia Nesterova, William Johnson, Amedeo Modigliani, Frida

Kahlo and Diego Rivera, Max Beckmann, Roy DeCarava, Josef Koudelka, Helen Levitt, and dozens of other artists. I definitely saw Haitian art, and one of my favorites was Fritzner Alphonse, but it was   just a part of everything else.

I basically developed my technique by painting all the time, continuing to practice. As I mentioned earlier, I did a few semesters of art classes in high school and college, but nothing major. I did the two semesters of the art major at La Guardia High and took a sculpture class at Cooper Union's Saturday program, which was really interesting and fun. After high school, I did maybe two or three sessions at the Arts Students League, some workshops at the International Center of Photography and a one-semester art class at Medgar Evers College.

To me painting was just [fun], not very technical. On the other hand, I recently took a printmaking workshop at the Bob Blackburn Studio, and there I obviously needed someone to show me how to use the materials. I like to start with an idea inspired by something that I see around me or that I've read or heard about. Then, I imagine what elements the piece should contain and create a [sketched study]. Sometimes, I'll sketch from life, other times I look in a print or electronic version of a book. For human figures I'll take a photo of a model, or look for interesting poses in images I see around me. So, it's a combination of using my imagination and things [in the real world] to make a piece.

I think what people see when they identify my work with Haitian art is the African Diaspora connection, which is most definitely there!

JW: Growing up, my mother told my brother and me that she wasn't as concerned with what line of work we pursued so long as we were committed and that it fulfilled us in some way. Did your parents set any professional goals that you felt you had to attain, or did you feel that it was open for you to decide?

LJ: I don't remember my parents being very explicit about what I should do as a career. My parents always worked from home, so I think I saw that they didn't go out to work, and that was an option too. They were generally busy people who didn't really sit me down to talk about anything. I think they [believed I was smart enough to] figure stuff out on my own. In retrospect, I think my parents were probably pretty typical of a lot of Caribbean people of their generation. Both of them were born in Antigua in the early 1930s—which makes me remember that they both have birthdays this month (November). My mother will be eighty-one and my father eighty-three.

I think my father had more advice when I became an adult and was doing my own thing. [He's told me that he] was pretty much on his own after his mother died when he was seven. He had a rough childhood in Antigua, which as far as I'm concerned was run like a plantation well into the twentieth century. He recently told me he was a sugarcane cutter from age thirteen to eighteen. This was among other odd jobs. He told me that he was very happy that he had work because, unlike his friends, he was able to buy a boat ticket to England before he was twenty[4]. [After coming to the States], my father worked as a laborer at Mt. Sinai hospital in Harlem, and then eventually got enough money to start buying houses in Brooklyn, places he says were dirt cheap and that nobody wanted. Since then, he's always worked in real estate. All of his properties are now in Antigua where he and my mother both live. He admitted for the first time a few days ago that he is getting old.

[4] *After World War II, many Caribbean immigrants settled in Europe. These migrants are often referred to as the "Windrush Generation," named after the Empire Windrush a ship that transported passengers from islands in the Commonwealth Caribbean to Great Britain.*

My parents were always doing something. Both worked extremely hard here in America doing all kinds of jobs that may have required more common sense and drive than they did book knowledge.

My mother came from a large, close-knit family. Here in New York, she did domestic work for a few families, and then worked as a nanny for many of our schoolteachers. Their kids came to our house which was across the street from the school. She also took care of my father, who didn't want her to go school or do any kind of office-type job because he insisted that she be home. I've never seen my mother in a pair of pants, and really think she handed my father her life on a silver platter. She wasn't a depressed person though, by any means, and always has a lot of people around her— her sisters and brothers, her children, and a lot of friends. She made wedding dresses and other kinds of clothes, baked, and made a lot of crafts.

My parents were always doing something. Both worked extremely hard here in America doing all kinds of jobs that may have required more common sense and drive than they did book knowledge. They are also very devout Christians and rigidly so. My father was terribly strict with his seven girl children and my mother. They were not lovey-dovey parents by any means, but I did always feel safe at home. We always had what we needed, if not what we wanted.

JW: In one of your YouTube interviews, you attribute at least part of your feeling of having freedom to choose your line of work to the fact that just as you were coming into adulthood, your parents moved back to Antigua and left a property for you there in New York. I'm sure that this freed you up in terms of "making the rent," but what were some of the other pieces of the puzzle that helped you feel comfortable enough to paint full time?

LJ: Well, since my parents worked from home, I saw how they ran their operations, so to speak. I never felt [obligated] to get an [outside] job, although I'm sure my parents must have said stuff about that, it wasn't impressed upon me in any real way.

I was the youngest of many children, and by the time I was eighteen my parents were a bit older than most parents of people my age. I felt they were a bit "over" taking care of children in a hands-on on way. However, I did feel that I had people to help me and to rely on, even if not my parents but my older siblings. So, [as the youngest perhaps] I felt that I could go out on a limb, because someone would be there if I got into trouble.

[From the business standpoint,] I was lucky to sell my paintings from the start so that was encouraging and I was also able to make money. Instead of waiting for someone to give me a show, I did it myself. When it came to organizing exhibits and showing my work, as well as others' work, the first show I curated was called *Njia Kuumba: Passages Through Creativity* in 1993 at the Ifetayo Cultural Arts Facility when it was on Flatbush Ave in Brooklyn (they are still around). I was twenty at the time. There were some pretty good artists in the show, a lot of them still making art.

I was also asked to participate in shows. The first show I was asked to participate in was at a place called Creative Concerns, which was run by Jacqui Woods who is now the director at the Skylight Gallery in Brooklyn, where I also participated in at least two exhibits. My first real solo exhibition was at The American Bible Society in 1996, and that same year I had another solo show at the Wright Gallery where they sold African art, both places in NYC. I also exhibited at Danny Simmons' Rush Arts Gallery a couple of times, and from that association I was asked to donate a piece to the Schomburg Collection where I was part of their *Black New York: Artists of the 20th Century* in 1999. So, there was always something going on.

JW: All of your video interviews on YouTube express how much storytelling plays into your work. Since so much of the African Diaspora story has been preserved in music, which ones (young or old) inspire you? Beyond musicians, who are some other painters, writers, etc. whose work feeds you? And what are you reading these days?

LJ: I love good music of all kinds. I have two "theme songs," both by Miriam Makeba, by far my favorite singer. The first one is "Uyadela," and the second one is "Umquokozo." I just love her voice! It's full of energy and life and emotion. I don't know what she's saying, but I just love the feeling it gives me. Even after hearing these songs a million times, I still get chills. It's like she's singing directly to me and telling me a story that I'm supposed to know. Also, as someone who likes to sing, it's just amazing what she can do with her voice. I also love Billie Holiday and Joni Mitchell, Sweet Honey in the Rock, Bob Marley of course, Fela and

John and Alice Coltrane, Don Cherry. My playlist these days has Dennis Brown and Gregory Isaacs, the Smiths, Soul Brothers, Jorge Ben Jor, Billie Holiday, and Miriam of course. All of this music is music I've been listening to for the past thirty years!

I like to read nonfiction. Right now I'm reading *The History of White People* by Nell Painter and *Sugar in the Blood* by Andrea Stuart. Not exactly cheerful themes, but I learn something on every page; it's truly incredible how much information is at our fingertips.

JW: When thinking about your family line—what you've observed directly or stories that have been handed down to you—do you see your work ethic, your dreams, your creativity as being an extension of work begun in some previous generation?

LJ: I draw on my experiences and stories people tell me, in my secular work especially; whether from family and personal history, or from something that I learn about externally. With the sacred work, of course the themes in these images are derivative of age-old traditions, of which I do feel a part. I feel a part of something larger, a continuum I guess you could say. I am connected to my personal family history, but even more so to the family of enlightened people everywhere.

My work ethic comes from my parents. My parents did so many different things. I guess they were "typical" Caribbean people who [juggled many] different jobs. But I never got the impression that they hated their work, even though it was mostly hard work. Most of all—even as a child—I knew they were reaping the benefit, as opposed to working for someone who would ultimately get the best of their labor.

In terms of work ethic, I also admire Marcus Garvey and Booker T. Washington. "MAKE WORK" is posted over my desk and is something I strive to do every day not just for me but for others too. I've recently initiated two projects to promote Bronx artists that will launch next year.

JW: How does your family feel about what you do? Do they see your work as legitimate, and do you see your children following in your footsteps?

LJ: My family is completely supportive of what I do. I think that's mostly because they don't have a choice! It's what I've been doing since I was eighteen, so they've all met me working as an artist. Yes, they do see the work as legitimate, because it works for me.

However, I think my children also understand there is a lot of hard work involved [in making art], and also many ups and downs. They are all already creative people, and I'm sure will be successful with whatever they do. My oldest is still trying to figure out what he wants to do with himself, but he's in college, so it's okay. He's begun designing and painting on clothing and is quite good. It's interesting that he's doing that now after years of me trying to steer them away from artistic careers! But I know that they have to do what they want, and

so I try to be supportive. My middle child is also in college. She's interested in publishing and writing of all kinds. I wish I could be like her when I grow up! She's a very thoughtful, brilliant young woman. My youngest is planning to study filmmaking in South Korea, teach English there, and live there forever! She's in the eleventh grade now and speaks Korean. She's in love with all things Asian, and I have no doubt that she will succeed in whatever she goes for! I encourage them to enjoy their work, because whatever it is, it's better if you actually like doing it.

JW: When you decided that you were going to earnestly pursue a living as an artist, did the idea of "folk" versus "fine" art ever concern you? How, if at all, did the fact that you are self-taught ever weigh in to where you felt you could go or achieve as a painter? When you first started painting, what was greatest aspiration for it?

LJ: Honestly, I just sort of went with the flow. Of course, I worked hard to make sure

I feel a part of something larger. . .
I am connected to my personal family
history, but even more so to the family
of enlightened people everywhere.

wherever the flow took me I would bring about the best outcome, but I didn't think too much about the art world or where I would be accepted.

Early on, three well-respected Black artists gave me advice. One said, "Don't do the Ethiopian art because it's derivative." Another one said, "Don't do secular work because everybody is doing that." The final one said, "Don't [waver between] both styles. Choose one, because otherwise people will be confused." So, from that I learned everyone has an opinion, and I should do what feels good to me.

There was another artist whose work I admire who was part of a panel at the American Folk Art Museum. He and two others were talking about self-taught artists. None of these people were actually self-taught, and I remember him saying "Self-taught artists don't agonize over '*the line.*'" This made me think about how I agonize over "the line" all the time, so what does that make me? Everyone is put into a category, and it's like a caste system. The best position for a Black artist is to have a degree from Yale or Harvard. However, that obviously wasn't

> *I didn't think too much about the art world or where I would be accepted.*

my path, so I just do what I do. Some people like it and some people don't.

In the past five years or so, with the [unstable] economy, new technology, etc., people are stepping out of the box more concerning the way to do things. Now, artists seem to be of the attitude that they will go with whatever works. I wouldn't say that I don't have aspirations for my work, but I don't sit around thinking, "Oh, I want to be in the collection at the MET or MOMA," especially because I know that curators associated with these museums don't just randomly choose who's shown there.

I always say if I waited around for certain people to notice my work I would have been working at the post office a long time ago. I respect postal workers, but my point is that [if I'd been too rigid in my expectations] I would have given up on art a long time ago.

JW: What kind of environment do you create for yourself when you paint—windows open to the world or no distractions, music or silence? And do you work steadily throughout the year or save the bulk of it for some set period?

LJ: Music, or some kind of white noise is a must. I listened to over forty audio books while painting [for] *Anna [Carries Water]*, and it was glorious. Also, I like to listen to nature sounds like birds or rainstorms. This is another reason to love the internet. I visit YouTube, Netflix, and Hulu a lot.

I paint best on a deadline and am good at tuning everything else out when I paint. I use little tiny brushes and it's mostly tedious and slow going. Deadlines are a good thing for me to have to make sure the work gets finished! I like to work on several pieces at once so if I'm not feeling one of them I can move on to the next.

JW: What message do you want your entire body of work to convey?

LJ: This is a hard question, because I work with a few different themes: sacred art, [the day-to-day struggles] of nannies and other domestic workers, race and slavery as well as mundane subjects. Ultimately, I want people to see something beautiful, even if it's a [tough] subject.

Beyond that, I love when a viewer personally identifies with something they see in my work; human beings share so many of the same experiences, no matter the long list of differences we're supposed to have.

"Guardian Angel," Laura James

Hold on to what is good, even if it is a handful of earth.

- Pueblo Indian blessing

Wendy E. Phillips
Documentary Photographer

From music and dance to food, folk medicine, architecture, and language, Latin America has an intimate relationship with Africa. Mexico is no exception. There, some of the points of entry for blacks were the northern states of Coahuila and Chihuahua, where members of the multi-ethnic Seminole tribe settled after the Trail of Tears. Toward the southwestern curve of Mexico are the neighboring states of Guerrero and Oaxaca, both on the Pacific coast and which contain what is known as the Costa Chica. Veracruz lies just opposite on the Gulf of Mexico. These three southern regions are known as places where the Afro-Mexican presence has taken firm root.

Photographer Wendy Phillips, thirty-five mm in hand, searches out these Afro-mestizo communities and ways of life. A native of upstate New York and long-time resident of Atlanta, Dr. Phillips' photographic work has been exhibited in group and solo exhibitions throughout the United States, Mexico, Spain and Portugal. Her most recent *La Sombra Series* explores the way that "the soul, or shadow, becomes lost or endangered [and] must be 'caught' or 'called back' to its owner so that equilibrium may be restored and to make healing possible."

The following interview occurred on May 27, 2004, at Dr. Phillips' studio, a group space near Emory University.

JW: Tell me about your beginnings and what you dreamed of being when you were a little girl. Did you think you'd be a photographer, an artist?

WP: When I was growing up black people who wanted to be upwardly mobile thought about being doctors or lawyers, and I wasn't sure that that was something I could do, though I knew of people who did those things. I decided when I was in grade school or high school that I wanted to be a physical therapist, and that's the first training that I actually did which has ended up being related to my work as, in a broad sense, a healer.

As I reflect, there were times that I was introduced to people who were artists, but it just never seemed like something that someone like me would do. That may be related to societal expectations or family expectations, and I say that in the sense

that for my parents education was valued. I think for many people of their era who lived through some of the Great Depression, this was the case and so was doing what was going to be consistent or reliable in terms of helping you to get a "good job."

JW: So what convinced you that art was something within your reach?

WP: My parents implanted rudiments of being an artist in that my mother introduced me to her friends who were artists and businesswomen. One woman was Jewish and had a business of putting together kits of textile work, embroidery work, and at that time this was pretty innovative. This woman rented warehouse space, and she would search for the yarns and the patterns and put all these things together and ship them out as her own enterprise apart from her husband and her family. And then another good friend

My parents implanted rudiments of being an artist in that my mother introduced me to her friends who were artists and businesswomen.

was a weaver; she was a black woman who, according to my mother, had survived having had a bad husband and a lot of children but bought these looms that she loved. You know, things that didn't really "make sense," weren't really "logical." But I know that this woman won prizes and was well-known in upstate New York for her weaving. Margaret Carr was her name. My mother took me to another friend of hers named Mary who was a watercolor painter; she took me to Mary's class and to Mary's studio.

My mother was pretty open to supporting whatever I might have wanted to try. For instance, I was interested in ceramics, and so my mother bought me a potter's wheel that was in the basement for me to experiment with. Then, my father's sister was a painter, and I know that in our house we had her work. She was a schoolteacher, but she was very serious about her painting.

JW: Growing up, what part did travel play in your education? Did your family do much exploring inside or outside of the States?

WP: Not real far-away travel. I traveled with my mother after I'd gone to college. We went to Arizona together, and there the art of the indigenous people—the jewelry and all those things—were crafts I was drawn to. We traveled to Puerto Rico. But when I was growing up mainly it was that we would take trips to Canada, especially in the summer because Rochester, where I grew up, was close to the Canadian border. And so, it wasn't a far-away country and place. We would go to Montreal, but more often we'd go to Toronto.

There was a national exhibition in Toronto that was like a world fair. Every year people would come from all over the world and they would present their cultures, and visitors could see slides and sample food. There would be exhibits. Toronto is a very multicultural city; people have retained their traditions within their neighborhoods. You know, you can go to parts of the city like Chinatown and learn much about Chinese people, etc. It gave me exposure to cultures, without having to go far away. We would go to close, overland places. My mother was very interested in traveling. She just didn't get to do it a lot.

In high school I often was friends with exchange students. I had a good friend from Buenos Aires, Argentina one year and another year a student from Finland who was there my junior year of high school. When the Finnish schoolmate eventually went home, she asked me to come to visit. At that point, I'd never gone much farther than Toronto. I finished my high school credits early, but my mother wouldn't let me graduate, wouldn't let me go to college early. She was really concerned about me being mature enough to take the next step.

But she let me not be in school, and so I decided to go visit my friend in Finland (laughs). I figured out how to get a ticket. My mother flew with me to New York, and I flew on to Helsinki alone and clueless. I was either sixteen or seventeen, seventeen probably because my birthday is in March. Some of the things I've done, I don't know that they were very cautious or rational (laughs).

I remember that I met this black man on the plane, and he was the only black person I saw the whole time I was there. I saw him on the street later on. It was weird being away from home alone for the first time, but it was also culture shock. Granted, in the town I grew up in there wasn't a huge black population. Still, Scandinavia was very different. I was there for about three weeks. Not a really long time. Again, I was drawn to textiles, and there was a lot of knitting. Scandinavia was where I learned to knit which is another thing that I do that I've been pretty obsessed with at different points in time. These women taught me to knit, and there was all this wonderful wool and colors and designs. There is a different sense of design in Scandinavia. Lessons were getting in there even though I was struggling in a place that was so far from home.

Then my friend from Argentina and I decided we were going to take a trip to Canada by ourselves after graduation. At the time I'd had this pen pal from England since about sixth grade, and my English friend was traveling to Ottawa to visit her sister. So, my friend from Argentina and I were going to travel to Canada and see Toronto and go on to Ottawa. She couldn't get a visa, so I decided to go by myself. Those were the first farther away trips that I took.

The next trip I remember was after my sophomore year in college. One of my friends was a black woman who'd grown up in Europe, because her father worked for the US government, and Germany was where they were living when she came to college.

We traveled throughout Europe on the train. That was interesting. One, because she grew up in Europe, and there were a lot of things that she didn't have reservations about in terms of safety, expectations of racism. She was ready to go. I was just a lot more cautious because I had these expectations of physical danger. This was '78. It was right after [the Spanish dictator] Franco had died. There was terrorism going on in Italy, but it wasn't anything that would change your decision to go someplace or do something. There wasn't much fear of being held up and all the things you'd be concerned about here.

The other piece was how we were perceived as these two "exotic" black women traveling alone, which to many people was so strange. There were people looking, asking where we were from, particularly in Italy and Spain. Fortunately, we could talk to most people. My friend spoke English, French, and German, had learned Italian, and remembered it once she got back there. I spoke Spanish and English. So we had a sense of what was going on. Still we were perceived as exotic and were traveling alone. Something about it was odd. Some of it was men being obnoxious. I hadn't experienced anything quite like that before. I remember talking to people about us being from America, discussing politics in Spain. My friend was more knowledgeable and aware

of why people were closed or hesitant to talk about things that were political. She'd wanted to go all the way to the South of Spain to Morocco and back in a short period of time. We only got as far south as Madrid (laughs).

Much later and in another verse in a similar song, I'd planned to go to Ghana with a friend. She ended up being in the midst of a divorce, and it was a bad time in her life. I asked other friends who'd been there and they said that it was really safe, and so I said that I would just go by myself. I went to Kumasi, to the Volta Region in the East, to Cape Coast Castle.

My husband doesn't always like it, but he has never said, "Don't go." With the Ghana trip, which was in '96, my kids were still pretty young. My daughter was ten and my son was seven. I've traveled by myself since then, but it's been to visit friends. On my next trip to Mexico I'm thinking about also going to Belize.

JW: How many children did your

parents have?

WP: I was an only child, and when my mother had me she was older. After she passed, we found out that she was older than she acknowledged. She had me when she was like thirty-six. That was really odd at that time. She would tell stories about how when she was in the hospital the nurses were coming to look at this "old" woman who had this baby. My mother was a point of great interest because she was different to have done that. She worked while she was pregnant, hiding the pregnancy so she could continue teaching, which is *not* something that people would do at that time. She breastfed me; that was *not* something recommended at that time. She definitely heard her own drummer.

JW: How did your formal training in physical therapy lead you to embrace photography?

WP: Physical therapy is related to my art in that I still do some of that work, mainly with women in the Latin community, Mexican women. Several of them have turned out to come from communities of African descent in Mexico. Now that they know me, we talk about their traditional practices and rituals. I've been collecting oral histories with them. And so, in the context of helping with their children and their families, they trust talking with me about things that are interesting to them. I'm planning to go in December to spend time with one woman's mother in a community that seems to have retained Yoruba and other African-based philosophies and rituals and healing practices. So, it's kind of all come together.

The other piece is that I've been studying some traditional Chinese medicine, which really is art if you think of the way the body is represented in terms of sketches of acupuncture points and the relationship that the Chinese draw between the human body and nature. It's just very, very beautiful.

JW: What ways do you feel your work to be

I've been really curious to know what the belief would have been, what would have influenced my beliefs and philosophy had my ancestors been allowed to continue to practice their own belief systems.

a continuation of that which your parents began?

WP: I think about how my mother had her classroom. It was very creative for a kindergarten. All this stuff going on. I would go after school to help her, and sometimes she'd have a rabbit or turtle, a tortoise living in her classroom. It would have its cage, but it might be out for a lot of the day with the kids. She played piano by ear. She would have different songs that would let her students know what was going to happen next during the day. She would do mixed media projects on her bulletin boards or windows. She really was doing her thing as an artist, as a kindergarten teacher. My mother would take me out to the woods to identify wild plants and bring them home and plant them in our house and we'd look them up in books. And she would take me to the library.

Those sorts of educational rituals gave me an example which I see is reflected in my work. A lot of what's important in documentary work is just to present an image so that someone can begin to think about how things came to be the way that they are. To me the educational part, trying to encourage people to think about history is an important part of my work.

I choose to work with the Latinas in the community, people who generally don't have many resources, because that was always my mother's choice. My mother was the first black teacher to be hired by the Rochester Public School System. They asked her where she wanted to teach, and she chose the least enfranchised neighborhood because she said she felt that it would be a good place to put her energy. I share that philosophy. She worked with migrant workers, teaching educational and health programs for their children in the summer. Most of these migrants were black people from Gullah areas of the South who came North to harvest crops.

My father was someone very interested in literature. He loved poetry, loved to recite poetry. Very interested in history. He wasn't studying our diaspora, but history was something he was very interested in.

JW: When did you first pick up a camera?

WP: Kodak is based in Rochester, so a lot of my relatives worked at Kodak. There were always samples of film and things around. I can remember Polaroids being in the house. At that time, cameras weren't something that I was really into. I remember in high school I'd grown really interested in the dark room and photography, but I didn't know if that was the thing for me. And so I never did photography there. In college there was a brother who was a photographer and he would do portraits of people, of me. It was a little business, a way to make money. I was kind of interested in the process of black and white photography. When I traveled with my friend from Germany we took snapshots, but nothing beyond that.

Probably the first time I started seriously taking pictures was around '86 or '87. My husband wanted a camera, so I bought him a thirty-five millimeter that he never got to use because I got so involved with it. I was working in a hospital, and there was a man who was a photographer who worked as a clerk as a day job. I would talk to him and have him critique my work. I was doing some black and white photography then. Then I put the camera down, went back to grad school.

Later when I moved here to Atlanta and my kids were dancing with Ballethnic Dance Company, there was no photographer, and I wanted pictures of them dancing. I went and asked friends about how to shoot theatrical work because, for instance, you can't use a flash when you're shooting dancers. It's dangerous and you could blind them momentarily and cause an accident. So I learned technique by doing my own research and started working for Ballethnic. I was their company photographer for four or five years.

After I started to work with the dance company, if we went on a family trip I was shooting more seriously. We took a trip to Mexico with the kids. I still have black and white work from some of the ruins. I began to approach photography differently there. In 1998, I decided to take a class in documentary photography in Mexico with Mary Ellen Mark, a very well-known documentary photographer here in the States, and a Mexican woman photographer named Graciela Iturbide in Oaxaca. Also, I took a class with Manuel Alvarez Bravo at the *Centro de Fotografia* in Oaxaca. It was very intense, a real push forward in terms of improving my work and approach.

JW: Do you find your subjects or do your subjects find you?

WP: A lot of times when you're working with a camera, being by yourself is a good thing. Being a black woman is like the least threatening thing for people when you go to their communities. They don't assume that you're going to harm anybody. They don't assume any bad intention. Being by myself and being a morning person means that all I have to do is go out and take a morning walk; people come up to me and talk to me, invite me to go to their house. So, it's really a gift. When I'm with my husband, people don't assume any potential harm either. But in some cultures people are a little more cautious about how a man would perceive something. When I'm by myself that's not an issue. They don't feel at all threatened, and also I know that I'm safe. There are problems in terms of someone who might take pocket change. But nothing in terms of violence, assault or things like that. One woman said, "Nobody has anything really, so why would anyone go out of their way to take it from somebody?" I have had to work to let down defenses of having negative expectations of people. I ask God to lead me to good people and good places. I keep that in mind. It's happening always. Always, always happening.

I remember being on the coast in Chacahua out walking early one morning

Wendy Phillips at the Basilica of Our Lady of Guadalupe, Mexico City

and the fishermen, who fish all night, were coming home. One Afro-Mexican man said something like, "What would bring this beautiful creature to our town?" The same line that you might hear downtown here! That was just his way of starting conversation. I can appreciate cultural similarities between people of African descent.

In Mexico, people often keep their animals near their homes. Once I was out taking pictures and there was this pig that was the biggest I'd ever seen in my life going down the road. I took a picture of it quickly before it changed its mind. Then a woman came out and I thought, "Oh no, I've insulted her somehow by taking a picture of her pig." No! She just saw that I had a camera and invited me to come have coffee with her, take a picture of her grandson.

Usually if I go to a place and I'm interested in photographing somebody, I'll talk to them and ask if I can. A lot of times I take a Polaroid camera and I give people pictures. People often don't have access because photography is expensive. Polaroid materials are very expensive. In one town in Mexico, the word was out that I had a camera. Within twenty-four hours people were coming up and saying, "Come and photograph me. Can I trade you fruit? What can I give you?" The

picture I took of the barefoot women standing beside a little girl with a beautiful dress, those people just appeared from behind a wall, around a corner.

JW: You're drawn to religious and spiritual imagery, and obviously in these places where you go to photograph, people have strong belief systems to buoy them and help their traditions to remain intact. How would you describe yourself spiritually?

WP: I grew up in Presbyterian and African Methodist Christian traditions. I would say that that's the base of my belief. However, in the last few years, particularly, I've had very close friendships with people who are non-Christian. I have problems with the aspect of Christian belief that says those who are not of that fold are not spiritual, the condemnation of other traditions.

My kids went to Quaker school, and my daughter decided after middle school to go to Quaker meeting as her spiritual place, and I ended up going with her. That's a place that's

In a heartbeat, I'd buy an airline ticket before I'd go to a one-day sale.

comfortable for me right now because of the non-judgment of other people's traditions, because of its pacifist orientation, its history in the abolition [of slavery in the US]. Actually, [while doing genealogical research] I learned that one of my enslaved ancestors escaped to a Quaker community. So it could be that generations back some of my people were of that tradition.

Some of the imagery I create is an exploration of what has been condemned in terms of traditional African spirituality and belief and has been deemed non-compatible with the major religions. I've been really curious to know what the belief would have been, what would have influenced my

beliefs and philosophy had my ancestors been allowed to continue to practice their own belief systems. That's one thing that I've learned from the women of African descent in Mexico. They've kept many rituals that to me are things that help you get through life. One of the traditions that the women from Mexico told me about is called the second funeral. The year after the person dies, there is this acknowledgment of them again and a ritual to help them move on to the next world. There are also healing rituals. One of them is called a *limpia*, a cleansing using herbs and an egg. In many ways, to me, it is related to energetic work and some of the practices of the Chinese. So it's not that it's so disorganized or apart. It's spiritual and philosophical. I've learned some of those rituals from the women. I received a *limpia* from an Afro-Mexican woman who was the aunt of a friend of mine, and it was very emotional because had not the repression and subjugation been so strong, that could have been my grandmother or my aunt doing that for me. But they couldn't because they weren't allowed to *know* anymore. This Afro-Mexican woman did. In terms of energy work, it was very relaxing but also very emotional to receive this from someone who did remember. The interesting thing about those women is that they don't recognize themselves as being of African descent, not because of a denial of culture but because Mexico has a big problem with this aspect of history. These women come from places of disenfranchisement, little access to education. So, many people just don't know.

JW: There is a fine line that an anthropologist or researcher walks between not imposing views on people, honoring who it is that people feel they are and at the same time recognizing that there are markers that clearly reveal ancestral roots—markers such as how people eat, worship, or think, what kinds of music they make that might be in some way obscured beneath the way they look. This is compounded by the fact that, particularly in Mexico, it seems that there is a loss of memory, and as you said not necessarily a denial of a connection to Africa. When I look at, say, Bobby Vaughn's Afro-Mexican website, Tony Gleaton's work, or at some of your images I sometimes wonder what makes you comfortable with classifying some people as Afro-Mexican, since sometimes the connection is something that we can't necessarily "prove" or is not the way that they might refer to themselves.

WP: There is proof in the sense that there have been anthropologists who have done work in this area. One is Aguirre Beltrán. He worked in some of the communities of the Costa Chica, talking to people about philosophical beliefs. But he also went into the Spaniards' records; they kept very detailed records about where people were brought from. He was able to speak with much support about where the ancestors of the people of that region came from, because he had the slavery records. My experience there makes me see something like a Freudian repression. Some people know. Mexican people who have university education know. They may admit that there are African-descended people who live around Acapulco, but they don't want to acknowledge much else.

With the villagers I'm just cautious about what I say, because there's some shame associated with some of those practices, having the sense that they're not everybody else's beliefs or practices. One belief is about totems or animals and that a person's spirit is related to an animal spirit in the wild. If something bad happens to the animal, then the person becomes ill. Those are very unusual ideas compared to what many may think about as explaining the causes of illnesses that people have. It's important that this is related to indigenous American beliefs too. These people are a mixture of the Africans and the indigenous people who didn't die in the genocide when the Spaniards arrived. I'll say to my friends, "Well, you know, those ideas are very similar to what some of my ancestors believe." The ideas are similar to those of people who live off the coast of Georgia or South Carolina because they've kept to themselves [and as a result have succeeded in keeping] their rituals and traditions.

Now, for some of the Afro-Mexican women it's almost like a sense of pride in [their ancestral] beliefs. One woman who doesn't read or write asked me if I was going to write a book about this. If you don't read or write, then having a library isn't your priority, but some have a sense of the importance of something even though it might be very far from their own experience. It's important to keep these things that the older people know about.

JW: Do you think they see any part of themselves in you even though you, for instance, have dreadlocks and probably speak Spanish with an accent?

WP: My hair wasn't always like this when I was traveling. People in Mexico will ask me where I'm from. I'll say that I'm from the United States. And they'll ask, "Well before you went there where did you migrate from?" That's very powerful. In many places I get that.

In Cuba, people would come to me on the street and ask directions. They would yell up to the balcony. People talk to each other from the balcony to the street. And there's a two-tier payment system for Cubans and outsiders. If you're not from there you pay more for a cab and to go into cultural places. The only time I was busted was when I was in a cab, one of those really old cars, and the guy had ornately decorated his dash and I asked to take a picture. He wondered why I

would want to [unless I was a foreigner] and made me pay the full fare. The women I was with were incensed, and said that they were getting out of the cab and weren't going to pay him a penny more. All of the rest of the time they told me not to talk, because my Spanish accent is like a Mexican accent. And then, Mexicans here in the States ask me if I'm Brazilian or Cuban.

The people on the Costa Chica refer to themselves as *moreno*. It has to do with physical characteristics and asserts that they are above and beyond all else Mexican. So I guess there's not much of an identification with me because people aren't thinking about that base. The people there are so isolated from the rest of Mexico and are so close to one another that they know everybody in their community. I went to one community twice; they went and got the man I'd had a conversation with the year before to come sit and talk with me. They know who belongs and who doesn't.

But there isn't a reference to this common root with me. People don't necessarily make that connection.

I've asked people where the *morenos* come from. One young woman told me that they came from Cuba. A lot of old people that I've run into tell the story of a shipwrecked slaver. Apparently, people tell it all along the coast. One woman said to me, "They say that they stole us away in slave ships." This is probably what people have handed down. The younger ones may know a little bit about slavery and that it existed, but they don't know that it's related to them. This is in contrast to Peru. There, in one small town, we visited [in the 1990s] we were sitting in the middle of the town, and people were observing us and trying to be respectful of our privacy. I asked someone where a store was. He [ended up offering] to have a meeting of the town where he would introduce us to the community. These were black people, a black town. He was talking about what was happening with [apartheid and Nelson] Mandela. I don't even know where people were getting the cable link! They were very aware. We went to another town in Peru, the one where I took the picture of the woman with rollers in her hair. She told me right away that she was so glad to have black visitors, that she loved it when black people came to her town, that the last people who came were from Haiti and they were so black and it was so beautiful. There was really this identification. These people are not intellectuals. They are farm workers, just regular folks. In another place people stopped us in the street to ask us to participate in this ritual of passing a cup to drink. They had this wine made of grain alcohol. They asked us to please come and pass the cup. Two times that happened. That was a ritual of welcome or acknowledgment. It was very clear, their understanding of blackness and the Diaspora. They told us that they refer to Cuba for their music and that strong music came from there. That was what they liked. In Peru the black people were not as isolated and you could take a bus to a larger town that would be only thirty minutes away. But where the people live in Mexico is so remote. Imagine that remoteness, which probably started off as a desire to be apart historically, combined with not having access to education.

In a Mexican family that I've gotten to know pretty well here in Atlanta there is a young man in his twenties. He once said to me that if he lets his hair grow then African Americans always greet him. He couldn't figure out why. My experience is that these *morenos* have this appreciation of the way they've been received by black Americans.

JW: So how do the people react when they encounter this Third Root idea or when they come to your exhibitions and see themselves framed as Afro-Mexican?

WP: Well, it's really hard to get people to come. Going to a show is so different from their experience. One time a friend of one of my friends was cooking traditional empanadas for my exhibition at Auburn Avenue library. I thought she was surely going to come out to see the photos after work. She didn't. I know now that I have to physically go get them.

We did a project at the Woodruff Arts Center called "The Changing Face of Atlanta: Documenting the Lives of Workers from Mexico." I kept asking the people whose faces were featured in the exhibition, "Are you coming?" At the last minute I had to go get them in my car. They said they couldn't believe that what they said [had been typed and put] on a wall. I'm sure it was very empowering, but it was hard to get them to go to a place, even there in Mexico, where the class thing or the foreigner/outsider thing is an issue.

I discussed my upcoming National Black Arts Festival show with the woman whose mother I'm going to visit in Mexico. I said that I'm going to have this show and it's about all the *morenas* that I've met in different places

I've been, that I feel the power in the images, that I put the work on the walls in my studio for the curator to come see and that I was a little worried about whether it was the kind of show the curator wanted to have. There was such power coming from the women in the pictures that I had to surrender and say, "If it's right, it's right. If it's not, it's not." My friend said, "So, when you go to my village, then you'll take my mother and my grandmother's picture and you'll put them in your next show." I'll go get this friend for the exhibit during the National Black Arts Festival.

When I visit Mexico, I tell people that I'm looking for my relatives and that I'm interested in finding other people who look like me in other countries, and that makes sense to them. The people look at my skin and my hair and say that I am a *morena*. But there's still something that's seen as being degrading about being part of this group. They might say something like, "*Somos morenos*," meaning "We're *just* morenos."

Sometimes I'll say to one of my friends that people were also enslaved in Mexico just to see where she would take that, since from Aguirre Beltrán's work we know that African descendants stayed along the coast of Oaxaca, Guerrero, and Veracruz. But Mexico enslaved people throughout the country. Now Veracruz is different; there are people who were originally enslaved but there was a lot of migration from Cuba and other parts of the Caribbean, and Tampico is near Veracruz. But in the Yucatan there are people of African descent, though something I recently read attributes that more to later migration. I gave a talk at a diaspora conference at DePaul University called something like "Representations of the Black Body in Mexican Visual Art: Evidence of an African History or a Cultural Myth?" Because when you go and look you find—another time I'll show you—that there are murals that depict slavery and liberation in Guanajuato state.

There are a couple of documentary portrait photographers such as Agustín Casasola who have photographed people over time, since abolition and onward and over a couple of generations in Guanajuato. Beautiful, beautiful portrait work and in it you see clearly that people are of African, indigenous and some European descent.

In Mexico City, I saw people and thought, "How could you *not* be looking at me [as family] when you look like that?" Here in Atlanta I went to the home of the neighbor of a woman from [an Afro-Mexican village] and she was such a strikingly beautiful black woman. I wondered why she wasn't in *Essence* magazine or something. I read something by a Mexican man who said he was harassed more by the police in Mexico who thought he was a foreigner. When he got here where there were a lot of black people, he was just one of the group.

JW: Financially speaking, how easy is it for you to be consistent with your travel and photography?

WP: I make money to do my photography by [providing physical therapy services to] families who have children with disabilities. And I sell my photographic work but not enough to contribute to our family income.

Opportunities have just come—like the Afro-Cuban filmmaker friend I mentioned earlier. He sent me an e-mail inviting me to write a proposal about documentary work and submit it to the university in Salamanca, Spain. We did and he wrote back saying that they accepted it. They are giving me a ticket to come and will pay for a place for me to stay.

Sometimes I've not had enough money to print pictures, and I have a friend who did expert printing for me for free. With my last show at Georgia Perimeter College I was trying to figure out how I was going to get that together; the woman who I share studio space with said that there are frames available for me to borrow, and they came and framed the work. And in the last couple months I've sold some pieces without even having had a show. So I haven't always had to figure out how to have enough to do these projects. I've experienced that by acknowledging my gifts God keeps things going. I'm learning that I don't always have to know exactly how situations are going to work out.

I began to learn that lesson when I was doing my dissertation at Georgia State University when I was interviewing women from St. Helena in the South Carolina Sea Islands as well as ones from Chattanooga, Tennessee and Sierra Leone, West Africa. My project was challenging. I was driving back and forth to St. Helena and Chattanooga, getting very little financial support, not to mention that there were attempts to repress and control my writing. At this time, my husband was basically paying for my field work from our family budget. I had the ability to earn more, but I had to stop to be able to write and get my dissertation done. So it's been a matter of looking at what's practical. There have been times when I've made more money than he has or vice versa. It has fluctuated.

The first time I went to Costa Chica I wasn't even sure that I was going to be able to take any money out of the ATM when I got there. What I'm learning now is that I must do things that are important to me. I can't wait for someone to give me money and a job and tell me to go do it. My husband and I were talking recently, and we said that we wanted to be able to retire and live someplace else. I don't know what I'm waiting for. I need to start trying to figure out how to make that happen. I can't wait for the academic job that offers me the sabbatical, though it may happen.

JW: Have there ever been times when all your roles as artist, traveler, mother, wife, and scholar have not meshed very well?

WP: Sure. For one person to take care of the kids when two people usually do it is not an easy thing. It hasn't always been stress-free, but we manage to get it done. My kids just know that there are certain things that I do, that go along with who I am. At one point it was hard to say that my interest was valid. For example, to want to buy a good camera when the money could be spent on something else. My husband was the one who would encourage me to buy equipment to practice my art. It was just hard for me. Then I had this period I went through of buying things that were really pretty shallow. Like designer handbags (laughs). At one point, I started taking those things to consignment shops. I took a bunch of those handbags and sold them. That's how I got cash to go to Africa. I had a fancy watch and sold it to a friend's cousin who's a jeweler. I took that money and bought a good camera. It was all a process of moving on. When I started doing that, my husband joked and said that people who have problems do this kind of thing. I buy clothes when I travel because I like stuff like this [referring to her embroidered Mexican dress], but they're not expensive. I don't buy clothes at the mall. I just use [my resources] in a different way. In a heartbeat, I'd buy an airline ticket before I'd go to a one-day sale. My husband and I have done home renovations over time, but we don't have fancy furniture. These things are not a priority.

JW: If verbally translated and taken as a whole, what statement do you want your work to make?

WP: Where I am right now is that I want it to tell the truth about what the Afro-Atlantic slave trade was about in terms of its magnitude and its impact on we who are the descendants. To help people stop making it less, repressing it, or forgetting about it. For us to know about each other.

Untitled, Wendy Phillips, 2001

In the late eighteenth century, Spanish leader Esteban Miró who governed the Spanish province of Louisiana, amended the Black Code to include what became popularly known as the Tignon Law. It required all women of color, enslaved or free, to wear head scarves or risk punishment. In response, many of these women put their design skills to work by creating elaborate wraps largely inspired by their African and Caribbean relatives. With these eye-catching creations that were sometimes made of madras cloth and accented with feathers, brooches, or other embellishments, they bestowed beauty on what was meant to be a mark of shame.

Gloria Rolando

Filmmaker

Since her beginnings in film over thirty years ago, Gloria Rolando has remained one of the few, if not only, black Cuban women behind the camera today. Rolando's formative years were steeped in culture and arts, partly because of being born in Havana's Chinatown barrio as well as because of attending music conservatory in high school and earning a university degree in Art History. Her documentaries show how the spiritual, as it intersects with the cultural and political, shapes the lives of everyday blacks. Beyond simply celebrating the black presence in Cuba, Rolando examines the many streams of the African Diaspora that have converged in her country, bringing to the surface bits of history that have, for one reason or another, been suppressed.

Her film *Oggún: An Eternal Presence* pays homage to the Yoruba deity of iron and remembers the contributions that singer Lázaro Rós made to the tradition of Afro-Cuban praise song. The short film *El Alacrán* and its longer companion, *The Marquises of Atarés* reveal the Congo roots and significance of neighborhood *comparsa* bands that parade during Carnival. *My Footsteps in Baragua*, tells the migration tale of a community that came to Cuba from the English-speaking Caribbean and the similar *Cherished Island Memories* explores the settlement of Cayman Islanders on the Isle of Youth just off of the Cuban mainland. *Eyes of the Rainbow* draws parallels to the goddess Oya and the life of Assata Shakur. *The Jazz in Us* shows the influence that African American musicians had on the minds of Havana youth and the common culture affirmed through the art of jazz in the years before the US trade embargo. Her most recent films are *1912: Breaking the Silence* and *Reshipment*. The former film elaborates on her earlier film *Roots of My Heart*, both of which document the killing of a group of men called the Independents of Color. The latter covers the lives of Haitian cane cutters deported from Cuba upon decline of the nation's once-lucrative sugar industry.

Throughout the span of Rolando's career, she has held the attention of a small but devoted global audience. Recent tours have taken her to South Africa, Canada and the United States. In summer 2012, she was a fellow with Colgate University's Robert Flaherty Film Seminar. The following spring, she and other notable artists of her medium showed her work in three American cities as part of the Cuban Women Filmmaker's US showcase and later that year during Stanford University's "Visualizing the Caribbean" Program.

I conducted the following in-person interview in April 2001 after the screening of her film *Raices de Mi Corazon/Roots of My Heart* during Georgia State University's "Cuba Today" symposium.

JW: Your work shows beauty and delivers a message, one case in point being your new film, *Roots of My Heart*. It puts a fictional family's daily life and historical tragedy side by side. Why did you feel that this approach would be more effective than documentary?

GR: Initially, I did want to make a documentary about the massacre of 1912, but I live in Havana and I work with few resources. Maybe I could have done the research, but would have had difficulty transporting the crew to the eastern part of the island. Cuba is large, and transportation is expensive. This could have created a lot of logistical problems, so for that reason I decided to work in Havana and create a fictional history. Even if it was still somewhat difficult to create an atmosphere specific to the story, approaching the project in this way made it easier to manage. But of course, a documentary would have been very interesting, but it would have required a lot more time for field research: like talking with old people in the countryside, checking facts, and so on. Information you get at one house may lead you to another to find someone. It's a long process. I didn't have the resources or time to do it that way.

JW: What was the urgency and why did you feel that now is the time to tell this story?

GR: I thought that it was important. This grew from my studying Cuban history, my interest in black roots in Cuba and the desire I had to reveal this side of the Cuban history. Yes, I think that all of the projects are urgent, are an emergency (laughs). Right now I have other projects in mind, and for me they are emergencies. Now is an opportune time for us to seek more comprehension about these matters. As Aline Helg [panel participant who delivered a paper titled "Race Relations in Cuba"] said today, we are now better able to sort through and talk about things that really were very painful. These pieces of history are ones that people really didn't know very well. Our research of the 1912 Cuban massacre was a challenge because not much literature has been written about it.

JW: In what ways do you see your work as being the same as and, then too, different from what is being produced in other parts of the African diaspora?

GR: I think that we have many things in

I think that we have many things in common. The problem is that sometimes the recognition is not there. African Americans do not know Afro-Cuban history, and Afro-Cubans also are not aware of how many elements we have in common with African Americans.

common. The problem is that sometimes the recognition is not there. African Americans do not know Afro-Cuban history, and Afro-Cubans also are not aware of how many elements we have in common with African Americans. The different countries had different processes of colonization, different patterns. There are many things that are constant in the African Diaspora. We share a lot of common ground. Our families, our ancestors, all of them were enslaved and they had to struggle to retain their culture and make society look upon them as respectable people.

JW: Specifically, in terms of film, there are many storytellers here in the US who are part of a black independent film movement. What aesthetic sensibility do you feel you share with people like them?

GR: We are all trying to find a language. Like Haile Gerima, we are trying not just to talk and tell the history, but to find and transmit the essence. Our way includes a lot of imagination and myths. We use a lot of symbols and music, the African music—in my case, the Afro-Cuban music. You know, these things are what permit us to create a kind of language, an aesthetic, where the music, history and everything are melded. We don't separate history from myth. Because in Africa, part of the history was not written and is not written. It is in the collective memory. I think that it is very important to include this memory in our telling of history. This way many people can connect with it. People can say, "Oh! This could be my history. This happened in my family." Or, "Yes, it's true, I think I feel something in common with this." Our task as filmmakers is to help create this kind of language.

JW: How does being an Afro-Latina shape the ways that you approach your work? Do you feel that your perspective is slightly different from any of the other black filmmakers because of this identity?

GR: No, not at all. As I said, we have many things in common. But this is a difficult question, because we do live in different countries, have different cultures, and the societies are organized differently. The way that society is organized is totally different in Cuba, not only because of the revolution. It's just because of the overall history. Because Cuba is both a Latino country and a Caribbean country, we share both of these perspectives. There are many elements that do create divisions. For example, many people in Cuba—even black people—have adapted certain cultural manifestations that belong to Mexico and other Latino countries like Peru or Puerto Rico. People would be surprised how closely we identify with some cultural elements that are common in those Latino

Gloria Rolando on location, *Reembarque* (2014)

countries. But also, we are a Caribbean country that contains many histories. Many migrants arrived in Cuba from Barbados, Trinidad, and all over. We have many black people in Cuba with English names. This is the topic of my documentary *My Footsteps in Baragua*.

JW: What made you become interested in these immigrant communities?

GR: As a filmmaker, I'm naturally inclined to study. You could have the best tools, the best cameras, but if you don't know the history and you are not interested in what happens around you, then you don't understand the importance of the tools. What are you going to express? You don't have anything to say to the rest of the world. So, the foundation that we have in history and knowledge about the world in which we are living is important. You must use these to re-evaluate your culture. I engage myself in studying the literature of the Caribbean, Cuban literature, know the patterns, know the histories. We need to open ourselves up to the world.

JW: Did your parents' outlook on the world influence this sense of connection you feel to the world or would you say that it was mostly due to your own curiosity?

GR: Of course my parents had a lot to do with it. It was curiosity, but was also a process of maturity. I received a lot of general elements from the university, in terms of general history. But there was much that I discovered on my own. I am a product of my family, my relationship with the world, the studies that I did. Everything is connected.

JW: What process do you go through in delivering your projects from idea to finished product?

GR: First, I study the topic I am going to present. It's a long process between examining the history and drafting the script. I have to determine what part of the story I want to focus on, develop my idea, then pinpoint what I would like to express and how I am going to express the idea. What is possible?

For example, I knew from the beginning with *Roots of My Heart* that I was not going to be able to deal very much with the fashions of 1912 because my budget was small. I had to think creatively about how I was going to reconstruct the period. I eventually came up with the idea to approach it using flashbacks that showed Mercedes' great-grandparents. Only the great-grandparents would dress in the costumes of the period. Nobody else. With the other people who appeared in the massacre, it was abstract. For them, I used old clothes from a film we made a long time ago about slavery. It was not necessary for their clothes to be exactly identified with one century or one period. Dirty, old clothes with holes were enough.

For me, what was important was the images of the blacks, that they looked beautiful and that they looked attractive. I said to myself that if I could make this history very human, maybe the viewers would feel the pain more, the destruction of the family, the way this massacre affected a particular black family. Basically, I go through the same process as every other filmmaker. I separate the film, hire a cinematographer. The common process. But the most important part is the conception, determining what I would like to show and developing the script.

JW: Family is essential, particularly in African and Latin cultures. How do family and work co-exist in your life?

GR: There are no divisions for me. My work is my life; it is built into my lifestyle. I'm very close with my mother and my grandmother.

My family is very proud of what I do. I have no children, but I included family pictures in the film. In *Roots of My Heart* you could see my mother's wedding, my father who died a long time ago, my nephew, my brother, my sister, my grandfather, my great-grandmother who passed two years ago. She was a big inspiration to me because she was a poor black woman who cleaned white people's homes before the revolution. She was proud of all of us because we made careers for ourselves. We became professionals. But for me, her history—even parts that I don't consciously know—is very deep inside me. Also, in the photo sequence of the children appears a photo of me and my sister when I was sixteen and my sister was around ten or eleven.

My family understands my commitment. My mother supports me. I am suffering right now because I can't contact her. On April 4, my birthday, I sent an e-mail message telling her "Thank you for giving me forty-eight years of commitment. You don't know the world,

I'm naturally inclined to study. You could have the best tools, the best cameras, but if you don't know the history and you are not interested in what happens around you, then you don't understand the importance of the tools.

but the world knows you through the pictures that I've included in [*Roots of My Heart*]." And I sent to her forty-eight flowers, one for each year that I've been on this planet, in this life. Now that I am married, my mother and I don't live together anymore. But when we did, I used to sit with her at night—even if she was sleeping—and share my thoughts with her. "Mamí, I think this," or "Mamí, I would like to do this." All the dreams I have I share

with her. So, the relationship I have with my mother and my grandmother is strong. The relationship that you see Mercedes has with her mother in the film mirrors the one I have with mine.

My mother also helps me make my films. Do you remember the scene [in *Roots of My Heart*] where a woman appears in a blue blouse? That belongs to my mother, because we didn't have much budget for costumes.

> *There are no divisions for me. My work is my life; it is built into my lifestyle. I'm very close with my mother and my grandmother. My family is very proud of what I do.*

Also, my mother dyed some of the garments that Mercedes' great-grandmother wore under her lace dress. She dyed the clothes at home because I told her, "Oh Mamí, I need to get the right blue color for this costume." With tremendous patience and love, Mamí dyed the cloth until it was the color that I needed. Maybe other people are not as close with their families, but family is important to me.

JW: Filmmaking is not typical "woman's work." How, if at all, has machismo been enacted in your country or elsewhere to hinder your progress?

GR: We need to change these kinds of questions. That question belongs to the twentieth century. We are now in the twenty-first century, and the situation has changed a lot. Women can do anything that it is possible to imagine. It all depends on your education, how well you focus, and your knowledge.

JW: What is the ultimate purpose of your work? To educate? To enlighten? To document the present and the past for the next generation?

GR: Opening the lines of communication is important. An art that does not communicate anything is not an art. I like making the sacrifices necessary to do my work. If you were to come to my house you'd see that it's very humble. Back home, I knocked on the doors of so many people and asked, "Could you lend me some of your furniture or fabric? I will take good care of it." It's the small things that help me. Of course, as a woman I like good clothes and fashion and everything. But, they are not my focus. Some people give incense, soap, or other small things. Gestures like this show that I have touched some part of a person's sensibility. And some people actually tell me this, which makes me very happy.

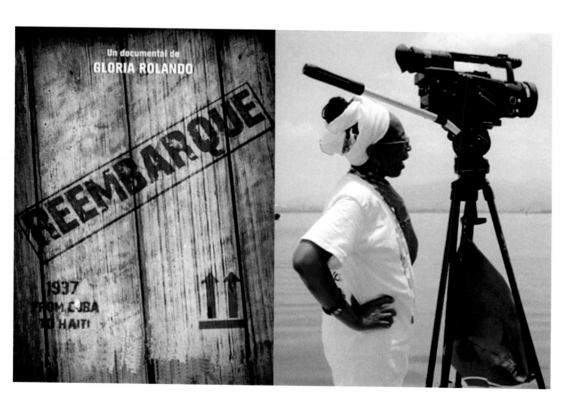

Gloria Rolando on location, *Reembarque* (2014)

*Honor her for all that
her hands have done,
and let her works bring
praise at the city gate.*

- Proverbs 31:31

In my parents' book and music library, circa 1976

Epilogue
My Creative Inheritance: An Extended Editor's Note

I was born in Galveston, an island-city on the curved dolphin's underbelly of the Texas Gulf Coast. In our love of food and family, we are the true kin of our port city relative, New Orleans. But what has always set the two distinctly apart is New Orleans' deep reverence for art, performance, and craft. On the family visits and getaways of my youth, I could feel the strength and power of the storied Congo Square bound tightly to the soul of New Orleans as well the spirits of her children. Everyone there seemed to proudly display some talent that had been nurtured, in large part, by a tradition of mentorship. The Crescent City was a place defined by freedom—of spirit and many times flesh—as much as it had been by enslavement. Art is so much a part of the frabic of southern Louisiana that it is impossible to hide it or restrict it to a corner of one's existence. There, art is the heart of life.

Texas has its own bold character and history which has become clearer and more fascinating to me over the years. But there were no portrait artists sketching in charcoal in the protective shade of Galveston's architectural landmarks like Sacred Heart Cathedral or Ashton Villa. Never did brass bands or Mardi Gras Indians, masked in feather-and-sequin finery, wind their way down Broadway or any of Galveston's backstreets. Nor were there young hoofers tap dancing and music making with improvised gear on the pavement of the Strand.

All this is to say that right alongside the joy that I found in the beach and the loving presence of my family, it was clear that in our neck of the bayou history had arranged things so that the social climate was (and remains) conservative in the practical consideration of how to earn a living and spend spare time. This was especially true for black people. Fortunately, by the Carter and Reagan years, around the time I was old enough to really take notice of such things, the days of the word "black" being synonymous with domestic or day laborer were largely bygone. It was becoming a little more common—though not commonplace—to see brown faces donning the many costumes of the union worker: nurses, mail carriers, telephone operators, truck drivers, petroleum plant workers, longshoremen, and teachers. Yet as far as I could see, few brown people seemed engaged the arts as a way to earn a living or feed the soul. Within my family I did notice a few exceptions.

My father was a kind of renaissance man. He was an enlisted military officer who left behind a small group of paintings after his and my mother's divorce. Daddy was proud that this work had won recognition in art shows while he was a cadet at the United States Air Force Academy, a school to which admittance was a feat within itself. I knew from stories and pictures that he was also a black belt in karate and an amateur DJ who invested a good deal of money in his sound equipment. Aside from Daddy, there were Mama's brothers. One of them was a mail carrier who loved to paint and who'd done a mural of the Resurrection that to this day remains a centerpiece in what was once my grandfather's church. Its flaxen-haired Jesus with his arms outstretched sprawls above the baptismal pool and was one of the things I'd study as this uncle and my aunts sang in the choir loft below, my grandmother embellishing their vocals with notes from her organ. Mama's youngest and probably most artistic brother had the raw talent of an actor and dancer. He died in the early 1990s while in his late twenties, and I'm convinced that he turned to a more self-destructive life path for lack of avenues or inspiration to fully develop his gifts.

As for the women in my family, I have an aunt who used to make beautiful Victorian doll houses and another who has always tended to her home with monastic care. And then there is Mama herself. From Day One, she gave herself heart and soul parenting. My brother and I were Mama's masterpieces, and my memory is full of examples of her marshaling every ounce of energy, imagination, and creativity to keep us well-nourished, neatly-dressed and most of all happy. She earned her living by working most of her life as a secretary and later as a paralegal. Young, intelligent and blessed with I'll-find-a-way-or-make-one tenacity, Mama filled our home with recorded music as well as a modest library of books, intentionally raising us in multicultural environments where we befriended an assortment of children born across the country and around the world. It's from Mama that I inherited a curiosity about life as well as the urge to write about what I saw. It was through her that I learned the old saying of the pen being mightier than the sword.

Of all the men and women of my childhood and young adult memory, there was only one who dared design her life according to her own vision: my grandmother Maggie. The historical record will undoubtedly list my grandmother as simply a housewife and mother of seven. Yet, within me lives the more complete story. She was a beauty who dressed with care when presenting herself in public yet who was camera shy. A straight-talker without a hint of pretentiousness. A woman whose inner mantra could well have been, "I'll do as I damn well please." A marvelous home cook and local celebrity fisherwoman who spent many mornings watching the sun rise on Galveston's saltwater piers. Very important to me is that my Grandmother Maggie was an artist in her own right. Since the moment in her childhood when she saw a piano sitting in the living

Grandma and Grandpa in church

room of a family for whom her mother was serving as midwife, my grandmother resolved that she would own one, too. Moving away from the tiny town of her birth and settling with relatives in big-city Galveston, she met my grandfather. After becoming engaged to one another, my grandfather Jewel bought my grandmother the first of many pianos. He knew and respected his soon-to-be bride's yearning to make music. Yet in the early years, Grandma had few opportunities to sit down at her piano bench to play a note because of the demands of caring for what steadily grew to become a large family. But she was patient. Some time after she turned forty—and after most of her children were grown and working out their own relationships with life—she returned to school to fulfill her dream. This pursuit occurred in the 1960s, during a time when it was customary to stay in one's place after it had been assigned. Yet rather than accept her lot, my grandmother regularly crossed the Galveston Bay and fifty miles of Interstate 45 to Texas Southern University to accomplish her creative goal. As my grandfather ascended the ranks of Southern Baptist ministry, Grandma Maggie walked alongside him treading her own course. Learning old stories like this and watching my grandmother practice for weekly choir rehearsal (as happened when we paid holiday visits) gave me my first glimpses of the interplay of self-determination and creativity.

While my grandmother's daughters admired her resolve, they didn't necessarily believe that everyone could or should follow the same path as their headstrong mother. In particular, for as far back as I can remember my mother encouraged to believe in and pursue my dreams, especially since she has always been a self-proclaimed dreamer herself. At the same time, during my high school and college years Mama constantly let me know that I had to square my shoulders, deal with reality, and "pay my dues." What was real was that we were working class black family living in the South. Texas, to be exact. Though I understood her point, the stubborn side of me sulked and bucked against her advice, hinting alarmingly as it seemed to that I should bury my aspirations. I feared that doing so for even a short time

Grandma at Avenue L Baptist Church, circa 1965

would kill my dreams—never mind that those hopes had yet to take on any solid shape. I think that Mama and our extended family hoped that a college degree and my love of stories would mean that I'd follow in the footsteps of Iola Johnson or Melanie Lawson, anchors who had integrated the local news. The problem lay in the fact that I was horrified by the blood-curdling events the news usually relayed and had an even greater fear of public speaking. Still, I majored in journalism when I enrolled at the University of Houston a few weeks before my seventeenth birthday, following the path visible from where I stood. It seemed the only way to go.

Since I'd worked on my high school year book staff, I was happy when collegiate newswriting assignments gained me behind-the-scenes access to my dormitory's dining hall (my intent being to expose, once and for all, the secret of why their food was so revolting) or opened the door to an interview with the busy pastor of the mega-church to which I at that time belonged. But ultimately my career as a student journalist was short-lived due to what instructors called my frequent editorializing and inability to grasp the fundamentals of rhetorical analysis and newswriting. While I absolutely agreed that I was not a "true" journalist, I knew that I was without question a writer of some stripe. What I couldn't figure out was what direction to train my attention and point my pen.

A turning point came when I enrolled in a black women's literature class taught by a playwright and scholar named Dr. Elizabeth Brown-Guillory. For this survey course, Dr. Brown-Guillory had assembled a reading list mostly made up of names that were foreign to me. Frances E.W. Harper. Dorothy West. Zora Neale Hurston. Paule Marshall as well as the popular fiction of Terry McMillan included for good measure. Though I had by this point sunken into a depression and become academically and emotionally stalled, I was inspired by Dr. Brown-Guillory's enthusiasm for her subject and warmed by the personal encouragement she took time to give me. In an attempt to redeem my grades, I took Zora Neale Hurston's *Their Eyes Were Watching God* along with me on my spring break vacation to south Florida vowing to finish it before my return home to Texas. I did, and like everyone else I swooned at this beautifully-written love story. But what struck me more profoundly was the Zora back story, her being a writer and cultural anthropologist, a discipline of which I had no prior knowledge and that seemed peopled by ones of my tribe. This discovery together with the ethnic mosaic and sensory pleasure of Florida—with its vivid blue skies, towering palm trees and the hospitality of my Belizean host family—began brightening my outlook on my life and future.

Back home, I changed schools and majors. I improved my typing speed, took classes in African American art, creative writing, and world religions. I became vice president of the campus' small Black Student Union and with a nod to Dr. Brown-Guillory, staged a night of dramatic readings of poetry from the Harlem Renaissance and Black Arts Movement. I was wholly engaged in my studies and had begun pursuing the arts and humanities in earnest; my much-improved GPA reflected my passion. I had an almost holy regard for Margaret Busby's *Daughters of Africa*, Susan L. Taylor's *In the Spirit*, bell hooks' *Sisters of the Yam* and just about anything written by Alice Walker. I was also a devoted listener of local public radio programs like *The Reggae Hall of Fame* and *African Kaleidoscope* which gave me passports to parts of the world that I began to dream of visiting. Encouraged by professors like Fabian Worsham who wrote glowing encouragements on my written assignments and Lorenzo Thomas, a Panamanian-American poet and lover of the blues, I began writing for publication. Mr. Thomas was very much to thank for this, since he invited to me submit one of my short stories to my campus literary journal. He also gave me my first paid writing assignment, a feature piece on a New Orleans music legend. In the semester before graduation, I got an internship at the jazz radio station that happened to air from the campus where my Grandma Maggie had studied music thirty years before. At KTSU, I wrote and occasionally voiced public service announcements and press releases and was taken under the protective wings of elder broadcasters like Rick Roberts and Maurice Hope Thompson. I also had the good fortune of meeting Danny Russo, a multi-talented visual artist and urban farmer who would become like an older brother and mentor. Danny's encouragement made me begin experimenting with photography, painting, music making, gardening, and vegetarian cooking.

By now I was seeing my way through the depressive haze that had cast deep shadows on my first two years of college and kept me from being able to envision my future. The light had come mainly through engaging the arts, a door to a vibrant world to which I now felt wholly, intimately connected. Often when I had extra time or money, I'd take the #77 bus down MLK to visit the Shrine of the Black Madonna. Sometimes I sat in on some of their Bible and history classes, and it was one of their members who introduced me to yoga. Always, I visited their bookstore and gallery where the floors and windows were polished to as shine and where there was always good music—be it jazz from KTSU, African, soul or reggae music on cassette. The smell—a combination of fragrant patchouli and myrrh—was always the same. The Shrine was a place at which I always felt at home and that always succeeded in inspiring me to dream. Most of the times that I visited, there would be the same cinnamon-skinned, matronly clerk on duty who was always pleasant whether I bought or simply browsed. One day as I sat cross legged on the floor previewing yet another book, she called out, "Sister, you teaching yet?" She asked this with a tone of certainty that I found bizarre since I'd never spoken with her about my personal life. I was open to possibilities and had in mind only a rough sketch of what I wanted to do after earning my degree. Her words did, though, give me something new to think about.

After completing my undergraduate degree, and because of the awakening that art gave me, I felt pulled to seek work in the bookstore of Houston's Museum of Fine Arts. Just before my hire, a wave of Frida-mania had swept through after their showing of *The World of Frida Kahlo*. I'd never heard of Frida, but her determined spirit was very familiar in that it reminded me in some ways of my grandmother. My new job required that I become familiar with the names of many other painters from different movements, as well as those of an international array of photographers, installation artists, sculptors, and architects. I loved my work environment and the opportunity it gave me to meet people from a range of cultures and social classes.

My most significant museum encounter came when the museum mounted *View from the Upper Room*, a retrospective exhibition of Dr. John Biggers, whose work I learned about during my last years in undergraduate school thanks to studying with Professor Floyd Newsome. Around the time of the opening, the museum put on a program, a panel on which noted art historian, Dr. Samella Lewis, the dashing Dr. Jeff Donaldson, and Dr. Robert Farris Thompson along with Dr. Biggers himself sat. While the erudite and theatrical presentation of Dr. Thompson was something I won't soon forget, Dr. Biggers captivated in a way that was more subtle. He was historian, storyteller and high priest with a paintbrush, laying out tales like none I'd ever heard. Dr. Biggers told of women as the first healers and keepers of time and did so in a raspy Southern voice that sounded as full of conviction as if he'd witnessed these wonders firsthand. Doc—the name affectionately given to him by his students and people in the community—was a regular at the museum bookstore. When he visited, he usually came around with curator and protégé in tow to scour the African art section of the store. Dr. Biggers' being warm and personable made all of the clerks rush to serve him. When my turn came, I paid attention to the types of books he bought. I especially remember Sylvia Ardyn Boone's *Radiance from the Waters* that dealt with the spiritual significance of the beauty rituals of Mande women in Sierra Leone. He would later insist that I read books by Dr. Charles Finch and Linda Beatrice Brown. Having glimpsed what was apparently his constant engagement with books and the way that the stories seemed to sharpen Dr. Biggers's vision and guide his hand, I gave him a copy of the spiritual autobiography of Malidoma Patrice Somé.

Being the founder of the Texas Southern art department meant that Dr. Biggers valued dialogue with young people, so when I requested an interview he obliged. During our conversation at a busy café near the museum, Doc shared a story about the power of language that he'd learned on one of his early trips to West Africa. When he invited me to read some of my work, I selected what I felt to be the worthiest of my poems. He listened and after pausing reflectively amid the piped in Dixieland jazz and din of others' clinking tableware offered this kindness recorded on my mini-cassette recorder: "I think you've got magic in your work. I really do. But you've got to boss it, you've got to beat it, you've got to train it." Doc knocked on the table for emphasis, before continuing, "You're going to refine your tools, and you will do that through struggle." He was echoing the sentiment of my mother and at the same time advising me of the challenge that would come from sustained engagement with my work. A short while later when I asked him to sign my *View from the Upper Room* catalog he inscribed it with another blessing: "Wishing you time, space and our Mother Ast" invoking one of the many names of Auset, the ancient Egyptian goddess of supreme creativity and empowered femininity.

Suffice it to say that as first my mother and then Dr. Biggers predicted, I have struggled in many ways and have invested many years in mastering, or *bossing* my craft. Part of my struggle has been to define and sustain myself as a teacher and a writer, to balance the creative pursuit with the imperative of taking care of my home and walking the long road to work stability. Alongside this and just like Mama, one of my proudest endeavors has been parenting my son with the best of what lies within me and to watch him grow into an inquisitive, creative, fully-realized being of his own. To earn a living, I have taught writing skills to college-bound youth, tutored at a two-year college, worked as a substitute teacher in elementary schools, given craft making workshops and cultural presentations at libraries, and occasionally sold my handmade

At Grandma's feet, Christmas 2002

crafts at outdoor markets and amongst friends. I have often held two and, during one stretch, as many as four gigs at a time.

Amidst the hustle, I have always tried to reserve time and what funds I could for indulging in activities that enriched my soul more than they ever would my pocketbook: doll-making, visiting ethnic markets and experimenting with recipes, roaming museums and hanging out in bookstores, container gardening and my primary outlet of writing. I also received scholarships to attend conferences and workshops sponsored by groups like the International Women's Writing Guild, Hurston Wright Foundation, and Yari Pamberi, all of which affirmed and enriched me. At the same time, I often felt anxiety and some guilt because of what seemed to be hard luck in securing stable, salaried work. This was especially true the older that I got and my own as well as my family's expectations of my settling into "real life" seemed especially pressing.

Some of what I dream, make, and do is meant to be shared only within my family—creations like collages, photo albums, letters, crafts to adorn my home. Then there are other projects that I want to share with a wider circle. Some I've seen all the way to publication, while others have been put on hold due to setbacks such as the major health challenge from which I had to fight my way back to strength and mental clarity, lack of funding or my simply doing what I had to do to keep up with the frenzied pace of life. In coming to terms with the latter, I have tried to summon the patience modeled by Grandma Maggie. I have also leaned on the assurance she would often give during our long-distance telephone conversations—she in her easy chair positioned within easy reach of her corded landline in her beachfront condo near the Galveston seawall, me reclined on the carpeted stairs of my apartment in suburban Atlanta. "Relax, Granny," she said during one of our talks, calling me by the nickname she'd crowned me with shortly after my birth. "You'll find your way." Perhaps said with such certainty because she knew that she had cleared it.

Lagniappe

More on Painting, Handcrafts, Photography, Theater and, Film

"Silence," Cannady Chapman

Beah: A Black Woman Speaks. LisaGay Hamilton (director). 2003. Portrait of Beah Richards, distinguished actress, writer, teacher, and social activist. Story is culled from a year's worth of intimate conversations between Richards and Hamilton who worked together on the film adaptation of Toni Morrison's *Beloved.* Note: Available online from Women Make Movies.

Behind the Scenes, or Thirty Years a Slave, And Four Years in the Whitehouse. By Elizabeth Keckley. Wildside Press. 2013. An illustrated memoir written by Keckley who used her dressmaking skills to purchase the freedom of herself and her son and went on to become the fashion stylist for Mary Todd Lincoln.

"Elizabeth Catlett: My Childhood" and "Elizabeth Catlett: Struggling to Get My MFA from the University of Iowa." Available on YouTube. Esteemed American sculptor and painter, who spent much of her artistic career in Mexico, speaks about defining moments of her life. Part of the National Visionary Leadership Project's oral history archive.

"Jeanne Moutossamy-Ashe." By Kalia Brooks. September 11, 2014. Accessible at bombmagazine. org. Online interview with trailblazing black American photographer, educator, and wife of the late tennis legend, Arthur Ashe. Discusses family; documenting the Gullah community of Daufuskie Island; friendships with other artists like Deborah Willis and mother and daughter Vertamae and Kali Grosvenor; and directing the Arthur Ashe Learning Center which "instills in young people the kindred spirit of imagination and creativity." Part of BOMB magazine's Oral History Project.

Lifestyle: The Artists' Way. Accessible on BET.com. A series of video shorts featuring interviews with artists like photographers Carrie Mae Weems and Deborah Willis and painters Kara Walker and Wangechi Mutu.

"Making Daughters of the Dust," in Daughters of the Dust: The Making of an African American Woman's Film. By Julie Dash. The New Press/W.W. Norton and Company. 1992. Iconic indie director recalls her chance introduction to the world of film at the Studio Museum in Harlem in the late 1960s. Charts key points in her career, namely writing, financing and filming cinematic gem titled *Daughters of the Dust,* a Great Migration story told mainly through the lives of three South Carolina women.

Viewfinders: Black Women Photographers. By Jeanne Moutoussamy-Ashe. Writers & Readers. 1993. According to art historian Naomi Rosenblum, *Viewfinders* is the first-ever book devoted to preserving the work of female photographers of any culture. Its pages offer a photographic survey of nearly 150 years of women contributing to the genre.

We Flew Over the Bridge: The Memoirs of Faith Ringgold. By Faith Ringgold. Duke University Press. 2005. Beloved children's book author, story quilt maker, painter and performance author recalls her life from her childhood in Harlem to her later years as a teacher in the New York City school system. Speaks candidly about many of her family relationships and recounts the difficulty of gaining entry into the world of art.

With Ossie and Ruby: In This Life Together. By Ossie Davis and Ruby Dee. Perennial/HarperCollins Publishers. 2004. A tale of love, and activism, this memoir visits important moments in the

The Spirit That Dreams

individual and married life of two iconic actors who committed themselves to their family, their community and their craft for over sixty years.

FOR CHILDREN

Art from Her Heart: Folk Artist Clementine Hunter. By Kathy Whitehead (author) and Shane Evans (illustrator). G. P. Putnam's Sons Publishing. 2008. Picture book about Louisiana-born menial worker and eventual artist who despite having created 5,000 to 10,000 paintings and drawings asserted: "I'm not an artist, you know. I just paint by heart." Story highlights her determination and resourcefulness in the face of many adverse conditions.

The Art of Miss Chew. By Patricia Polacco. G. P. Putnam's Sons Books for Young Readers. 2012. After watching her artist grandmother at work, Trisha, who struggles in school, decides that she wants to follow the same path. Her dream begins to take shape when she is one of the students selected to learn from Miss Chew, an Asian woman who dresses with flair, drives a sports car and is as skilled in teaching and standing up for the rights of students as she is at making art. A work of fiction drawn from the real life of one of the most prolific writers of childrens literature.

Drawing from Memory. By Allen Say. Scholastic Press. 2011. In this memoir in graphic novel format, the author recounts his early years as an aspiring artist coming of age in the tumult of World War II-era Japan. Say gives special attention to the value that mentors have on the development of their protégées.

Golden Domes and Silver Lanterns: A Muslim Book of Colors. By Hena Khan (author) and Mehrdokht Amini (illustrator). Chronicle Books. 2012. A visual tour that simultaneously teaches young readers about aspects of the Islamic faith as well as the world of color experienced within it.

Gordon Parks: How the Photographer Captured Black and White America. By Carole Boston Weatherford (author) and Jamey Cristoph (illustrator). Albert Whitman & Company. 2015. Picture book biography about pioneering artist and Renaissance man who triumphed over negative life circumstances and went on to made significant contributions to a variety of art forms, most notably photography and film.

Hands: Growing Up to Be an Artist. By LoïsEhlert. Houghton Mifflin Harcourt Books. 2004. Beautiful, simple picture book for very young readers about a child who, due to seeing her parents building, painting and sewing in and around their home, is inspired to do the same.

In Her Hands: The Story of Sculptor Augusta Savage. By Alan Shroeder (author) and JaeMe Bereal (Illustrator). Lee & Low Books. 2014. A fictionalized account of the life of Savage who migrated from rural Florida to New York and who, along with figures like Meta Warrick Fuller and Loïs Mailou Jones, would go on to become one of the most accomplished female visual artists of the Harlem Renaissance.

Jake Makes a World: Jacob Lawrence, A Young Artist in Harlem. By Sharifa Rhodes-Pitts (author) and Christopher Myers (illustrator). Harry N. Abrams. 2015. A glimpse of the early influences of one of the most famous 20th century African American muralists starting in "his mother's apartment, where he is surrounded by brightly colored walls with intricate patterns; to the streets full of familiar and not-so-familiar faces, sounds, rhythms, and smells; to the art studio where he goes each day after school to transform his everyday world on an epic scale."

The Magic of Spider Woman. By LoïsDuncan (author) and Shonto Begay (illustrator). Scholastic Books. 1996. In Navajo lore, Spider Woman was an artisan whose job it was to weave the fabric of the universe. From rugs and blankets to intricately woven stories, she taught people how to make life beautiful and showed them ways to achieve harmonious life balance. This picture book is a cautionary tale about one who ignores the important lessons offered by Spider Woman.

Maya's Blanket/La Manta de Maya. By Monica Brown (author) and David Diaz (illustrator). Lee and Low. 2015. This bilingual story tells of the many transformations made by a hand-made blanket after a grandmother hands it down to her grandchild. An adaptation of the traditional Jewish folk song-story "I Had a Little Overcoat."

My Hands Sing the Blues: Romare Bearden's Childhood Journey. By Jeanne Walker Harvey (author) and Elizabeth Zunon (Illustrator). Two Lions. 2011. A first person narrative tracing Bearden's family move to Harlem during the Great Migration and the part that his close connections to both the North and the South played on his development as a master visual artist and storyteller.

My Pen. By Christopher Myers. Disney Hyperion. 2015. Written by prolific children's book illustrator and son of acclaimed author, Walter Dean Myers. A warmly poetic book written for "the people who make things, and to the people who share them" in the voice of a young boy artist who finds a way to achieve the impossible in the worlds he creates with the help of his pen.

Painted Dreams. By Karen Lynn Williams (author) and Catherine Stock (illustrator). Harper Collins. 1998. Picture book about Haitian girl who, despite having many chores and responsibilities, wants to paint and finds inspiration in local artisans already pursuing the path.

Painting Dreams: Minnie Evans, Visionary Artist. By Mary E. Lyons. Houghton Mifflin. 1996. Nonfiction chapter book that visits moments in the life of self-taught North Carolina-born artist. Evans' dreams inspired her to draw and paint incessantly as she sought to share what she felt to be divinely-inspired depictions of nature, people of indigenous cultures and mythical creatures.

A Splash of Red: The Life and Art of Horace Pippin. By Jen Bryant (author) and Melissa Sweet (illustrator). Knopf Books for Young Readers. 2013. A self-taught artist, the child Pippin drew to entertain himself and the members of his community. When as a grown man he is called to fight in the Great War, his commitment to art is so strong that he continues at it even in the trenches only putting down his tools after being wounded. Calling on his will, spirit and patience, he heals his body, revives his creativity and succeeds in eventually becoming recognized a master of his craft.

Virtual and
In-Person Learning

Berkeley Rep School of Theater

http://www.berkeleyrep.org/school/

"The School of Theater's programs strive to stretch their students' imaginations, foster their creative potential, and encourage them as artists to develop the commitment necessary for artistic excellence."

California Newsreel

www.newsreel.org/

For nearly fifty years, California Newsreel has been a producer and distributor of "cutting edge social issue films for activists and educators." Lends and sells a wide variety of documentaries, dramas, comedies and classic films from the US, Latin America, the Caribbean and Africa for rent or purchase.

Center for Digital Storytelling

storycenter.org

Based in the California Bay Area, the Center for Documentary Storytelling works "with organizations around the world to develop programs which support individuals in rediscovering how to listen to each other and share first person stories. Our group process and the stories that emerge serve as effective tools for change."

Duke Center for Documentary Studies

http://documentarystudies.duke.edu/

Duke's CDS uses film, video and photography to connect the lives of people who live and work in everyday communities with those in university and uses this relationship "in advancing broader societal goals." Their manual, Visual Storytelling: The Digital Video Documentary (Nancy Kalow) is a free downloadable book "for anyone who wants to make a watchable short documentary using a consumer camcorder, digital SLR camera or cell phone."

Indiana University Black Film Center/Archive

http://www.indiana.edu/~bfca/home/

"The BFC/A's primary objectives are to promote scholarship on black film and to serve as an open resource for scholars, researchers, students, and the general public; to encourage creative film activity by independent black filmmakers; and to undertake and support research on the history, impact, theory, and aesthetics of black film traditions."

Living Ma'at: Creative Living Channel

http://www.livingmaat.com/

Launched by Ericka Taylor, Living Ma'at is a website encouraging the creative expressions of black women through "articles, interviews, resources, and products that inspire you...to live a just and balanced life." Its Creative Living section features "home decor ideas, highlights

The Spirit That Dreams

quick and easy craft projects, includes interviews with amazing artists and designers, sewing inspiration, jewelry making, and all the crafty creations in between."

Mayseles Documentary Center

http://maysles.org/mdc/

Located in Harlem, New York, the Maysles Documentary Center "is dedicated to the exhibition and production of films that inspire dialogue and action." Their Teen Producers Academy, Junior Filmmakers Summer Intensive and Film in Action Summer Camp are some of the programs through which they equip those interested with the tools needed to tell their stories through film and video.

MIT OpenCourseWare

http://ocw.mit.edu/courses/find-by-topic/

With MIT Open Course Ware, "[t]he idea is simple: to publish all of our course materials online and make them widely available to everyone." Their OpenCourseWare catalogue offers over 2,000 courses, some of them in Humanities and Fine Arts. Though the classes are not-for-credit, they offer a technical knowledge that can be used to establish an arts career or pursue traditional study.

Wonder Root

http://www.wonderroot.org/

WonderRoot "empowers artists to be proactive in engaging their communities through arts-based service work. [They] believe that art is an agent of change and that by empowering people with the means to create art, we are in turn empowering people with the means to create change." Wonder Root offers classes, tools and production space at reasonable rates.

Image and Quotation Credits

Cover model image used by permission of Jenissa Sullivan; **page 1**, (quote) used by permission of Rachel Elizabeth Harding and Duke University Press/Diane Grossé (Rights and Permissions); **page 5**, ©Rowan Heuvel/Unsplash.com/Creative Commons License; **pages 6, 22,** and **26**, used by permission of Eliciana Nascimento; **page 28**, used by permission of *Callaloo Journal of the African Diaspora*/Katy Karasek/taken from "An Interview with Louis Mailou Jones" by Charles H. Rowell, *Callaloo* volume 39 (spring 1989): 370; **page 29**, used by permission of the Loïs Mailou Jones Pierre-Noel Trust/Dr. Chris Chapman; **page 30**, photograph of Laura James © Janis Wilkins used by permission of Janis Wilkins; **pages 33** and **44**, "Self Portrait as Frida Kahlo" and "Guardian Angel" used by permission of Laura James; **page 47**, "Succulents" ©Folkert Gorter/Superfamous Images/Creative Commons License; **page 48, 59** and **71**, used by permission of Wendy E. Phillips, an abbreviated version of Wendy E. Phillips' interview appeared in the Spring 2007 issue of *Exposure*, the journal of the Society for Photographic Education; **page 73** used by permission of the Louisiana State Museum/Anna Gospodinovich (Rights and Reproductions); **pages 74, 80,** and **85**, ©Gloria Rolando/Imagens del Caribe; **page 87**, Hand of Fatima original design used by permission of Yesha Darji; **page 102**, "Silence" ©Cannady Chapman/used by permission of Cannady Chapman. **All interviews used by written permission of interviewees** and due diligence pursued to secure licenses/permissions for all photographs and illustrations.

Index